MW00593877

"If it looks like a Christmas book and if it sounds like a Christmas book, then it surely must be a Christmas book! But it's even more than that. *Let Earth Receive Her King* shows us how the Christmas story explains God's purposes from the dawn of time to the end of history. And it wouldn't be an Alistair Begg book if it didn't also show us how that story provides answers to the deepest needs of our hearts. Reading these pages will surely help all of us have a better Christmas. But I for one wouldn't be surprised if it helps some readers have their best Christmas ever."

SINCLAIR FERGUSON, Ligonier Ministries Teaching Fellow; Author, *Love Came Down* and *Union with Christ*

"There's no better or more faithful companion than Alistair Begg to widen your gaze and deepen your understanding so that you will be glad to 'prepare Him room.' These devotions are full of scriptural insight and refreshment that will enhance and enrich your Christmas season."

KEITH AND KRISTYN GETTY, Hymn-writers; Authors, *Sing!*

"In this just-right book for daily reading during the Advent season, Alistair Begg presents the compelling story of the need for Jesus, the coming of Jesus, and the beauty of Jesus that runs from Genesis to Revelation."

NANCY GUTHRIE, Bible teacher; Author, *Blessed* and *Even Better Than Eden*

LET EARTH
RECEIVE HER
KING

thegood**book**
COMPANY

Let Earth Receive Her King
© Alistair Begg 2024

Published by:
The Good Book Company

thegoodbook.com | thegoodbook.co.uk
thegoodbook.com.au | thegoodbook.co.nz | thegoodbook.co.in

Published in association with the literary agency of Wolgemuth & Wilson.

Cover Design by Faceout Studio | Art direction and design by André Parker

ISBN: 9781802541182 (hardcover) | 9781802541106 (paperback)

Printed in India

CONTENTS

PART FOUR: CHRISTMAS IN THE LETTERS

PART FIVE: AWAITING A NEW ADVENT

Joy to the world, the Lord is come!
Let Earth receive her King.
Let every heart prepare Him room
And Heaven and nature sing,
And Heaven and nature sing,
And Heaven, and Heaven and nature sing.

Joy to the earth, the Savior reigns!
Let all their songs employ
While fields and floods, rocks, hills,
and plains
Repeat the sounding joy,
Repeat the sounding joy,
Repeat, repeat the sounding joy.

(Isaac Watts, 1719)

INTRODUCTION

I love the Advent season. I love its sense of anticipation, and I love the way it takes me back to Christmases as a child—the singing, the church, the gifts.

I love the preparations, too. Some of us are the kind of people who start getting ready for Christmas in September. I am not one of those. I am more of a December-preparer. As a pastor, I find myself each December still writing my Advent sermons, and envying those who planned theirs out months earlier. My approach to gift-buying is similar. Thankfully, my wife is very much more of an organized person, otherwise things would be chaos.

It is easy to look at the first Christmas as though God were a December-preparer—as though the story starts on the first page of the New Testament, with an angel suddenly showing up to a girl in Galilee. But the Bible is a two-act drama, and to start at the Gospels is to join at the interval. No, God's preparations for the moment when this earth would receive its King started where

John's Gospel does: not with angels and shepherds and wise men, but "In the beginning"—in fact from before the beginning. From eternity past God planned to send His Son so that we might have life with Him for eternity future.

And so in these pages we will start at the beginning, and follow God's preparations for the awe-inspiring event of that first Christmas night. We will trace His plans and purposes through the Old Testament, before we enjoy reflecting once more on the events surrounding the coming of the Word made flesh.

But we will not stop there. "Advent" comes from the Latin word "Adventus," which means "Coming." And we are meant to have two "comings" in view—Christ's arrival in the past and His return in the future. The King of creation has walked on this earth, in history. And this earth will receive its King once again, this time arriving not as an unheralded baby but coming gloriously, unmistakably, on the clouds of heaven. Children, of course, spend Advent looking forward to Christmas Day. We are invited to look beyond that, and to a far greater day—the day Jesus returns. So our time together will start with Genesis 1, and by Christmas Eve we will have reached the other end of the Scriptures and the final chapter of Revelation.

This Advent, then, I invite you to join me in looking back to the Lord's first coming—to how the wondrous gift was given, and how that gift is joy to the world, and joy for our hearts, today. And I invite you to join me in looking forward to His second coming—to what God is still preparing to deliver in the future, and what that, too, means for us today.

My prayer is that these Advent devotions will cause you to wonder at all that God has done, and worship the one who lay in the manger that first Christmas night; and that they will foster within you a great sense of anticipation for Christ's return and prompt you to wait with joy for the day when earth once again receives its King. My prayer is that this Advent season, you and I would grow in our love for Him.

PART I

CHRISTMAS
IN THE BEGINNING

I. THE WORD IN THE BEGINNING

*"In the beginning, God created the heavens
and the earth."*

GENESIS 1:1

When we think about Jesus, it's inevitable that certain images come to mind—especially during Christmastime. It seems that we've largely moved past the era when most Western depictions of Him featured a blond-haired Jesus with striking blue eyes, holding a little lamb in His hands as He strolled through a blissful land where peaceful rivers flow. But although we may have left behind the idea of a blue-eyed, blond-haired Jesus, it may still be that most of our mental pictures owe more to artistic liberty than they owe to biblical theology.

It's striking that none of the New Testament writers—nor God Himself, as He inspired their words—found it important to describe Jesus' looks. All we know is that "he had no form or majesty that we should look at him,

15

and no beauty that we should desire him."[1] Why is such a description so conspicuously missing? Well, perhaps a key reason is that every human portrayal of Jesus misses what the Father desires for us to know about His Son. Even the greatest paintings and video productions will not allow us to conceive of Jesus in the awesome way in which He is introduced to us in John's Gospel, where we are invited not to wonder about how He might have looked but to wonder at His eternality, His personality, and His divinity:

> *"In the beginning was the Word, and the Word was with God, and the Word was God. He was in the beginning with God. All things were made through him, and without him was not any thing made that was made." (John 1:1-3)*

No matter how far back we consider the beginning of time to be and no matter what model we may have in our minds of how time began, there we will find the preincarnate Son of God already existing. "In the beginning," there was already God—and there was already God the Son, the "Word." John connects the dots to Genesis 1 for us. This Jesus was not created, for He is the very Creator of the universe. The child in the manger was the very same person who put the stars in the sky—including the very star which led the wise men from the east to come and worship Him.

---

1 Isaiah 53:2.

In His eternality, this Word, Jesus, is distinct from the Father and from the Spirit, not in essence but in person. He "was with God," yet He "was God." Both statements are true. Though it may sound puzzling, John wasn't writing in abstractions. He was presenting a person with whom he had laughed, wept, feasted, prayed, served, traveled, and far more—a person who nonetheless was also present at the creation of the world, as the Creator of the world.

It's somewhat obscured in our English translations, but John's use of verb tenses is masterful. He uses the imperfect tense (indicating an ongoing action) as he's describing the preexistent location of the Son: He "was with God, and ... was God." But then he switches to the aorist tense (indicating a decisive moment in time) when he says, "The Word became flesh."[2]

There was a point in time, over 2,000 years ago, when the second person of the Trinity, Jesus, who existed before time began, was delivered into this world like billions of other babies have been. That is what we call Christ's first advent and what millions celebrate each Christmas. There was a point in time when He obediently gave up His life to bear the penalty of our sins, and a point in time when His dead body came back to life, and a point in time when His resurrected body ascended into heaven. And there will be a point

2 John 1:14.

in time when this same Jesus comes again to make all things new.

⁘

Christ's divinity, then, has no starting point in time. He always was. He was God before time began. He is God at this very moment. And He will continue to be God forever.

If I am honest, I find it is easy to fall into the trap of spending each Advent season so busy with preparations that I do not dwell on the truth that the Creator became a creature and lived in this world. Perhaps you struggle with that too. There is a better way—not just during December but every day: "We are called to worship him without cessation, obey him without hesitation, love him without reservation and serve him without interruption."[3] To the extent that we ensure that we pause to gaze with the eyes of faith at the Word become flesh, we will find ourselves moved to worship, obey, love, and serve the Lord.

Christmas comes truly alive when we make time to think about the Lord Jesus. Remember, His physical appearance did not matter one bit—but, at the same time, enjoy the fact that He physically appeared, there at that first Christmas, to be our great hope in life and death.

---

3 Bruce Milne, *The Message of John: Here Is Your King!*, The Bible Speaks Today (InterVarsity Press Academic, 1993), p 36.

For Reflection:
How do the truths about Jesus' divinity and humanity prompt you to worship Him now?

> *Ere the blue heavens were stretched abroad,*
> *From everlasting was the Word;*
> *With God He was, the Word was God,*
> *And must divinely be adored.*
>
> *By His own power were all things made;*
> *By Him supported all things stand;*
> *He is the whole creation's head,*
> *And angels fly at His command.*
>
> *But lo! He leaves those heavenly forms;*
> *The Word descends and dwells in clay,*
> *That He may converse hold with worms,*
> *Dressed in such feeble flesh as they.*
>
> *Mortals with joy beheld His face,*
> *The eternal Father's only Son:*
> *How full of truth, how full of grace,*
> *The brightness of the Godhead shone!*
>
> *The angels leave their high abode,*
> *To learn new mysteries here, and tell*
> *The love of our descending God,*
> *The glories of Immanuel.*
>
> *"The Deity and Humanity of Christ"*
> *Isaac Watts*

2. THE FIRST PROMISE

"I will put enmity between you and the woman, and between your offspring and her offspring; he shall bruise your head, and you shall bruise his heel."

GENESIS 3:15

I'm sure you have heard and seen ads about celebrating Christmas in July, but have you ever given any thought to discovering Christmas in Genesis? Over the next few days, as we anticipate Christmas, we are going to do just that.

⁓——⌐

Genesis 3:15 provides us with what is often referred to as the *protoevangelium*—the first gospel. Good news was needed because God's command to not eat "of the tree of the knowledge of good and evil" was broken, and the promised punishment for such disobedience was death. The serpent had tempted the woman to distrust God—to doubt the words that He had spoken and to question the goodness of His creation. In no time, it would seem, the tree from which God had expressly forbidden eating became a "delight to the eyes" of the woman. Tragically, she then "took of its fruit and ate, and she also gave some to her husband who was with her, and he ate." And so Eve listened to the serpent, Adam listened to Eve, and nobody listened to God.[4]

Think of the evil one's scheme in the garden as it relates to your own life. You may hear about certain issues of the day that conflict with God's clear commands of Scripture and (figuratively) hear a whisper asking, *Well, why would it be necessary to obey such an arbitrary and unreasonable prohibition?* The lie of the devil is always the same: *I can make it possible for you to experience a better life beyond the boundaries of God's plan, and I'll make sure that you won't have to deal with the consequences.* But the truth remains that he can't and doesn't.

⌒

What is striking about the account of the aftermath of the first humans' great rebellion against God is not that death and banishment from the garden follow but that they do not follow immediately. Yes, those consequences and more would come in due time, but first came a divine promise. This reminds us of a wonderful truth about our God: undeserved grace flows from Him, even in the face of human rebellion. This amazing promise from God was that a seed—an offspring—of the woman would come to deal with this serpent—this great usurper who was in conflict with the very purposes of God. From this point in Genesis on through history, there is a war between the evil one and humanity, the pinnacle of God's creation.

The evil one was warned, even as humanity was cast out of the garden, that someday a male child who would undo his evil schemes would be born. From this point, every birth of a boy should have prompted the question, "Might this be the one God promised?" The devil's agenda was to make sure humanity never got to the "he" of verse fifteen. Hence Goliath against David, the Babylonians against Jerusalem, Nebuchadnezzar against Daniel, and many more examples throughout the Old Testament.

It's no stretch to say that Satan was trying with all his might to prevent Christmas for thousands of years—for what God's people mark as a day of celebration was surely, at the time, the worst moment of the devil's existence. Who else could have been behind Herod's design to destroy all the male children under the age of two? He was seeking to destroy that which God had planned. This enmity between the one whom God promised would bruise the head of the serpent and the serpent himself is the great conflict of human history; it is the underlying plotline of the whole Bible.

Unlike the devil, though, we can say to God, "I know that you can do all things, and that no purpose of yours can be thwarted."[5] Before man's relationship with God

5 Job 42:2.

was spoiled as a result of rebellion and before Adam and Eve were created, God had already planned the rescue. While the Bible gives no direct answer as to why God allowed the fall to happen, it does prove this: God is in control of all things. This is a cause for celebration if you long to live under the rule of the one who will make everything wrong come right.

Because God is in control, nothing could prevent the birth of that promised head-crusher of the serpent, Jesus of Nazareth. Because God is in control, nothing could prevent the perfect life that He lived. Because God is in control, nothing could prevent His triumph on the cross, when He bruised the serpent's head. And because God is in control, nothing can prevent the coming age when the serpent is totally defeated and God's great reversal is complete.

The baby in the manger at Christmas is the "he" of Genesis 3:15. We can rest in the reality that Jesus was, is, and always will be in control. We can remember that He will one day gather all who are His own and usher us into a new Eden. We can enjoy looking forward to the day when He will give to each of His people the privilege of enjoying eternal life with no sin, no sorrow, no sickness, no bitterness, no family divisions, no political wrangling—just never-ending beauty as we enjoy perfect communion with our Creator.

For Reflection:
In what area of life do you need the security and comfort of knowing that Jesus is and always will be in control?

What difference would it make to your view of the future to remember that one day Jesus will make everything wrong come right?

> *Creator of the stars of night,*
> *Your people's everlasting light,*
> *O Christ, Redeemer of us all,*
> *We pray You, hear us when we call.*
>
> *In sorrow that the ancient curse*
> *Should doom to death a universe,*
> *You came to save a ruined race*
> *With healing gifts of heav'nly grace.*
>
> *When earth drew on to darkest night,*
> *You came, but not in splendor bright,*
> *Not as a king, but as the child*
> *Of Mary, virgin mother mild.*
>
> *At Your great name, majestic now,*
> *All knees must bend, all hearts must bow;*
> *All things on earth with one accord*
> *Join those in heav'n to call You Lord.*
>
> *To God the Father, God the Son,*
> *And God the Spirit, Three in One,*
> *Praise, honor, might, and glory be*
> *From age to age eternally.*
>
> *"Creator of the Stars of Night"*
> *Latin hymn, trans. by John M. Neale*

3. WAITING FOR JESUS

*"Noah found favor in the eyes of the LORD ... Noah
was a righteous man, blameless in his generation.
Noah walked with God."*

GENESIS 6:8-9

"Are you ready for Christmas?" It's a question that
we hear quite often at this time of year! But the
first Christians would never have understood such
a question. For about the first three centuries of the
church's existence, Christmas was not a key celebration. (My Scottish ancestors kept this going for a lot
longer than that, but other more sensible believers decided in the 4th century that Christ's advent was worthy of deeper reflection.)

When the church began to celebrate Christmas, they
did so with a dual focus—both looking back to what
we refer to as the incarnation and looking forward to
the fact that this same Jesus, who had come as a baby
in Bethlehem in relative obscurity, will come again in
power and in glory. Thinking about this twofold reason
for reflection and joy raises a second (and more important) question: are we ready for *Jesus*?

We left God's first people with the promise of the one who "shall bruise [the serpent's] head," waiting for the child to be born who would reverse the effects of the fall. But the very next generation of humanity witnessed not salvation but murder. Mankind no longer needed a talking serpent because the prompting to sin was all inward, leading to division, murders, and revenge. Men and women were "drawn on by the inner reality of a destructive magnetism."[6] Sin spoils what God made good, spreads throughout humanity, and separates man from God and also from fellow man. Ten generations later, in Genesis 6, the corruption of humanity, in their hearts and in their actions, was so great that God resolved, "I will blot out man whom I have created from the face of the land."[7] The God who was and is in control, the God who fashioned the waters in the beauty of creation, determined to bring those very waters into place and use them as an expression of His judgment. It is quite devastating. This verse is not the kind of cheerful Bible passage that you'll want to include on your family's Christmas card. But Scripture is clear: God will execute His just judgment.

Yet it is also clear that, at the same time, our God is a gracious, merciful deliverer.

—⁓—

---

6 Alec Motyer, *Look to the Rock: An Old Testament Background to Our Understanding of Christ* (Kregel, 1996), p 127.

7 Genesis 6:7.

In the midst of corruption and on the cusp of judgment appeared one who "found favor in the eyes of the LORD … a righteous man, blameless in his generation." Noah, we discover, was a man who "walked with God." He knew who God was, and he trusted that God would keep His promises. Since he trusted, he obeyed. He walked with God.

You will know the rest of the story. When God warned him of what was to come and laid out how He would rescue Noah and his family, Noah obediently built the ark (which was approximately the size of one and a half football fields, so you can imagine how long that took). He built it one day at a time, fully trusting in God's word, waiting on and readying himself for His promised judgment.

Does that kind of faithful perseverance and trust in God describe you today?

Am I ready for Jesus? I may be ready for Christmas; the gifts may already be ordered and wrapped, the decorations might look like they belong in a Hallmark movie, and my social calendar might be full. It is tempting to focus on the things of this world, both the good and the sinful, perhaps more so in this particular season than in any other. But of far more importance is this: are we walking with God, so that we are ready for the second coming of Jesus, in salvation and in judgment? We don't know when that day will be, but we are told to be alert, to be patient, and to make sure we are ready.

Noah did not walk with God in perfection; nor will we. But that's okay, because Jesus Christ did. We have not been told that we need a wooden boat to find refuge from God's judgment. We have heard that we need a wooden cross, for His wrath was poured out on His only Son at Calvary. There, God displayed unfathomable mercy by placing His unimaginable judgment onto His Son. As we ponder Christ in a cradle this Christmas, we do so in awareness of what He accomplished on that cross.

> *Mercy there was great and grace was free,*
> *Pardon there was multiplied to me,*
> *There my burdened soul found liberty—*
> *At Calvary.*[8]

At the first Christmas, we find the better Noah, rescuing us from a greater judgment. One who walked with God. One who is God. The only one in whom we can find refuge and rest, now and forever. We walk with Him as we trust His promises and therefore seek to obey His commands.

For Reflection:
Are you ready for Jesus' return?
Are you struggling to obey Jesus in some way? What promise of His can you rely on, that will free and motivate you to follow His commands?

---

8 William R. Newell, "At Calvary" (1895).

Thou didst leave Thy throne and Thy kingly crown,
When Thou camest to earth for me;
But in Bethlehem's home was there found no room
For Thy holy nativity.
O come to my heart, Lord Jesus,
There is room in my heart for Thee.

Heaven's arches rang when the angels sang,
Proclaiming Thy royal degree;
But of lowly birth didst Thou come to earth,
And in great humility.
O come to my heart, Lord Jesus,
There is room in my heart for Thee.

"Thou Didst Leave Thy Throne"
Emily Elizabeth Steele Elliott

4. PROVIDING A LAMB

*"I will make of you a great nation, and I will bless
you and make your name great, so that you will
be a blessing ... and in you all the families of the
earth shall be blessed."*

GENESIS 12:2-3

Ten generations passed from the days of Noah to
the days of Abram (later and better known as
Abraham). After the judgment that came upon Noah's
generation, it would be reasonable to assume that it
was nearly impossible for Noah's descendants to forget
about the gracious refuge that God had provided in the
ark. But no...

Just as Noah's story had a dark background and then
a ray of hope, so too did Abraham's story. The darkness fell on the plain of Shinar, where mankind's pride-
ful rebellion continued in the form of their refusal
to treat God as God and to fill the earth as He had
purposed. "The whole earth had one language and the
same words," and they came together and said to one

another, "Come, let us build ourselves a city and a tower with its top in the heavens, and let us make a name for ourselves, lest we be dispersed over the face of the whole earth."[9]

Of course, the whole thing came to a crashing halt. Knowing the hearts and minds of humanity, God said, "This is only the beginning of what they will do ... let us go down and there confuse their language."[10] And so the Lord did just that.

Genesis 12, however, shows us another ray of hope. In direct contrast to those who gathered where they thought was best and wanted to make a name for themselves, Abraham was commanded by God to leave behind the land that he knew and to place his reputation (his everything, in fact) into God's hands. He was called to trust God's promise that "*I* will make of you a great nation, and *I* will bless you and make your name great, so that you will be a blessing."

Only God can make a name and a legacy truly great. And the melodic line that runs throughout the rest of the Old Testament is essentially this: in Abraham, "all the families of the earth shall be blessed."

In other words, God promised that the seed of Abraham would bring the blessing that was lost as a result of the fall. It was God who, in response to the tower of Babel, divided and scattered a humanity bent on defying Him. You may experience some of that division in your

9 Genesis 11:1-4.
10 Genesis 11:6-7.

own family this Christmas. You will certainly read of it in the newspapers.

And it is God who unites and brings together a humanity desiring to worship Him.

⁃——————⁌

There is an old movie called *The Gathering* that came out in the 1970s, and part of it was filmed near the church that I have pastored since I moved to the United States. It's about a dying businessman, who finds out he's dying shortly before Christmas and does his best to make amends with the family that he had abandoned years earlier.

I'll leave it to you to see how that plot unfolds. But the wonderful story of the Bible is that God is doing just that: gathering His people and making all things new. This was His purpose through the generations of Abraham's family—42, to be exact—until the first Christmas and the days of Jesus. Yet the chosen lineage very nearly came to a crashing halt before Abraham's son, Isaac, even had a chance to get married and have children. And astonishingly, it was God Himself who seemed to threaten the promises He had made to Abraham.

God told Abraham to take his only son, the one on whom rested the promise to bless families throughout the world by regathering them as God's people, and offer him as a sacrifice. This command was unvarnished; no explanation was given and no benefits were guaranteed. And yet still Abraham obeyed God, and "rose early in the morning" to begin his trip with Isaac. The faith in

God's covenant promises that had prompted Abraham to pack up and leave behind his old life enabled him to be obedient even in the midst of an inconceivable trial that threatened those very promises.[11]

After journeying nearly 45 miles with his son, on the third day, Abraham looked up and saw the mountain to which he had been sent: Mount Moriah. And as they moved closer, he surely anticipated the question that eventually came from Isaac: "Behold, the fire and the wood, but where is the lamb for a burnt offering?" Yet still Abraham trusted God: "God will provide for himself the lamb for a burnt offering, my son."[12]

As the story reaches its climax, with the son bound upon a sacrificial altar and the father ready to do the unthinkable because of his faith in and fear of the Lord, God intervenes, sending an angel to halt the sacrifice of Isaac. Abraham looked up and saw a ram caught in the thicket "and offered it up as a burnt offering instead of his son."[13]

Abraham had said God would provide a lamb—but instead He provided a ram. Isn't that a bit odd? Perhaps not. Perhaps Abraham's prophetic word was reaching beyond Moriah that day and into the cradle in Bethlehem, near where an angel would interrupt some shepherds watching their flocks at night. Those shepherds would leave their lambs to go and see another: "the Lamb of God, who takes away the sin of the world!"[14]

---

11 Genesis 22:1-5.
12 Genesis 22:7-8.
13 Genesis 22:13.
14 John 1:29.

And take away our sins is just what He has done. About 2,000 years ago, on Mount Moriah, God did with His Son what Abraham did not have to do with Isaac. On that day, God led His Son up the hill. On that Son's shoulders, the wood for the sacrifice burdened Him with a great weight. And on the cross, the Son was bruised; the Son was the sacrifice.

This is the story of salvation—the story of how "all the families of the earth shall be blessed," as God gathers a people who will dwell with Him in unity and harmony forever. What happened with Abraham can only be understood in light of the Christ; what happened in that manger can only be understood in light of the cross. God is now stretching out His hand and gathering people from every nation, by saving a doctor here and a college student there, a young child before bedtime and a great-grandmother on her deathbed. He saves people from every tribe, every tongue, and every nation. Think about how many millions will worship Christ this Christmas, gathering with God's people to sing praises to Him. Wonder at the fact that we will be among them. This is God's doing, in fulfillment of His ancient promise to Abraham, and it is glorious in our sight.

For Reflection:
How do the truths we have considered today make you marvel at God?
What difference will it make to you this Advent season to remember that unseen millions are worshiping Jesus alongside you?

Come, Thou long-expected Jesus,
Born to set Thy people free;
From our fears and sins release us,
Let us find our rest in Thee.
Israel's strength and consolation,
Hope of all the earth Thou art;
Dear Desire of every nation,
Joy of every longing heart.

Born Thy people to deliver,
Born a child and yet a King,
Born to reign in us forever,
Now Thy gracious kingdom bring.
By Thine own eternal Spirit
Rule in all our hearts alone;
By Thine all sufficient merit,
Raise us to Thy glorious throne.

"Come, Thou Long-Expected Jesus"
Charles Wesley

PART 2

CHRISTMAS
IN THE LAND

5. THE LORD REMEMBERS

*"The Lord remembered her. And in due time
Hannah conceived and bore a son, and she called
his name Samuel, for she said, 'I have asked for
him from the Lord.'"*

1 SAMUEL 1:19-20

If you have children, you probably cannot get through
a day during December without having cause to remember that Christmas Day is coming. Whether it is in
counting the number of Advent calendar doors remain-
ing or in the excited chatter about presents, or simply
in the way they hop from foot to foot as they talk about
everything the day will hold… it is hard to forget that
Christmas Day is on its way.

But of course, remembering the mere fact that Christmas is on December 25th is of little use. Imagine that
the morning dawns and you have made no preparations
and bought no presents. "I have remembered that it is
Christmas Day" is unlikely to soothe troubled young
hearts (and stop tearful young eyes) at that point!

No, truly remembering that Christmas Day is coming
means not just knowing it but acting on it. And so it

is in Scripture when we read that God "remembered." It was not that a person or a promise had slipped His mind and now He has recalled them. It is that He is now making good on a promise that He has made.

God promised to rescue Noah from the ark. And He remembered His promise, and the waters began to recede.

God promised to free Israel from slavery in Egypt. And He remembered His promise and called Moses to lead the people to the promised land.

When it came to Hannah, though, there was no specific promise.

<hr>

Hannah dwelled in the promised land a few hundred years after the days of Moses, and around eight centuries after God made His covenant promises to Abraham. During Hannah's time there was no king, and time and time again the people did what was right in their own eyes rather than what was right in God's sight.[15] They were in God's land, but they were far from God in their hearts. Because of their disobedience, the nation of Israel experienced instability and insecurity.

In many ways, Hannah's life was a microcosm of Israel's reality. She was a barren woman in a spiritually fruitless nation. At the point in the history of God's plans that she lived in, no child meant no ability to be part of God's plan of making Abraham's family

---

15 Judges 21:25.

into a great nation—of God's purposes in continuing to work through His people toward the day when His King would come, when the promised serpent-crusher would arrive.

We can imagine Hannah, in our terms, thinking on each New Year's Eve, *Perhaps next year will be the year when I fall pregnant*—but it never was. After years of feeling such deep anguish and enduring mockery from others, Hannah brought her deep affliction before the Lord in prayer.[16] And God "remembered" Hannah, and she gave birth to a son. When He did so, He was not simply answering one woman's prayers but drawing her into His plans—into the way He would keep His promises to Abraham. He remembered Hannah by acting to keep His promises.

Little did Hannah know that the child that she had been given, Samuel, was destined to become a prophet to the people, to call them back to living under God's rule and to identify and announce the king who would shepherd them well—King David. But God knew all that when He "remembered" Hannah. The answer that God provided for Hannah was part of His answer for the much larger predicament of His people. In the life of a no-longer-barren woman, the drama of God's redemptive purpose is unfolding before our eyes.

Again and again in Scripture, this is how God works—in humanly impossible ways and through unlikely people. Abraham's wife, Sarah, was barren,

---

16 1 Samuel 1:9-18.

but God intervened, and she bore Isaac.[17] Samson's mother was likewise unable to bear children, but God intervened, and she gave birth to a son who would in his death defeat his people's enemies.[18] And so here, Hannah could not have a child and yet did. In this way, God shows that the keeping of His promises is His work and His work alone—not ours. But He also shows that anyone can be drawn into His great plans and purposes, no matter how marginalized or maligned they may be. Whatever lies in our past or our present, we are never beyond being used by God to further His glorious eternal purposes. Now as then, God delights to reach into the humdrum, ordinary lives of His people and redirect the course of human history.

As we think of babies born to women who could not be pregnant, our minds should jump forward to the New Testament—not only to Mary, a virgin, but also to one of her relations, Elizabeth. Here was an elderly, godly woman who, like Hannah, had experienced years of barrenness—until an angel told her husband, Zechariah (whose name means "the Lord remembers"), that she would fall pregnant. Elizabeth's son, like Hannah's, would be God's means to "turn many of the children of Israel to the Lord their God, and ... to make ready for the Lord a people prepared."[19] Samuel had anointed

---

17 Genesis 21:1-7.
18 Judges 13.
19 Luke 1:16-17.

King David; and Elizabeth and Zechariah's son, John, would baptize King Jesus, David's greater descendant. In the gifting of this baby, God had, Zechariah realized, begun to "remember his holy covenant," for John was the prophet sent to announce the coming of the one in whom all God's promises are made Yes.[20] In the home of an aging childless couple, the drama of God's redemptive purpose is unfolding before our eyes.

God remembers His promises, and God remembers His people. He is always at work to establish His word and fulfill His eternal plan of salvation. He works in His own time, not ours—Hannah and Elizabeth could attest to that—and He does not promise to give each of us all of what we long for. But He does give us what we most yearn for: peace with Him now and a future with Him in which we will lack nothing, know no heartache, and need never shed a tear. He does, in ways that are not always immediately apparent, work *through* us to achieve His purposes.

So, as you look toward next year, you can be sure of this: it will be a year in which your God remembers you and is always working for your good. And it will be a year in which God graciously works through you, to bring His promises to His people and for His world to fruition when once more the Lord Jesus comes—this time, not in a virgin's womb but on the clouds of heaven. Just as Hannah was beckoned into the drama of what God is doing in His world, so too are we.

---

20 Luke 1:72; 2 Corinthians 1:20.

For Reflection:

How can the truth that God remembers you comfort you today?

Is there someone you know with whom you can share this truth and this comfort?

> *O come, all ye faithful,*
> *Joyful and triumphant,*
> *O come ye, O come ye to Bethlehem!*
> *Come, and behold Him,*
> *Born the King of angels!*
> *O come, let us adore Him,*
> *O come, let us adore Him,*
> *O come, let us adore Him, Christ the Lord!*
>
> *God of God,*
> *Light of Light,*
> *Lo, He abhors not the virgin's womb;*
> *Very God,*
> *Begotten not created;*
> *O come, let us adore Him,*
> *O come, let us adore Him,*
> *O come, let us adore Him, Christ the Lord!*
>
> *Sing, choirs of angels;*
> *Sing in exultation;*
> *Sing, all ye citizens of heav'n above!*
> *Glory to God,*
> *Glory in the highest!*

O come, let us adore Him,
O come, let us adore Him,
O come, let us adore Him, Christ the Lord!

Yea, Lord, we greet Thee,
Born this happy morning;
Jesus, to Thee be glory giv'n!
Word of the Father,
Now in flesh appearing!
O come, let us adore Him,
O come, let us adore Him,
O come, let us adore Him, Christ the Lord!

"O Come, All Ye Faithful"
Trans. by Frederick Oakeley

6. WILL GOD DWELL ON EARTH?

"Will God indeed dwell with man on the earth?
Behold, heaven and the highest heaven cannot contain
you, how much less this house that I have built!"

2 CHRONICLES 6:18

After Queen Elizabeth II died, many millions around the world tuned in to watch the coverage of her funeral. Around one million people packed the streets of London for the funeral procession. And about 2,000—including nearly a hundred heads of nations—filled Westminster Abbey to pay tribute to her life and character. You can imagine that every attendee will tell their children and their grandchildren, "I was there."

Similarly, it's safe to assume that people who were present at the dedication of the temple in Jerusalem would have spoken of it with wonder and would have done so for all their days.

Thousands of people were involved in building the temple during Solomon's reign. It took place over a period of some seven years; around 70,000 men bore burdens, 80,000 quarried in the hills, and 3,600 were engaged as overseers in the project. As it was being built, it was clear that no expense was being spared. It was gilded and displayed in magnificence, with carvings and with precious stones and overlaid with gold. King David had desired to build a house for the Lord, but God withheld that privilege from him and instead granted it to his son. So Solomon embraced it with a clear vision, saying, "The house that I am to build will be great, for our God is greater than all gods."[21]

We might think that at the temple's dedication, Solomon would have been saying to himself, *Can it get any better than this?* But instead, he asked, "Will God indeed dwell with man on the earth?" That's the big question. Great indeed was this temple for God, but was it great enough for the one whom "heaven and the highest heaven cannot contain"? Was it great enough to restore the kind of relationship Adam and Eve had had with God in the Garden of Eden?

Years of construction, no expense spared, tens of thousands involved in the project, a justifiable celebration of dedication in these moments, and at that point King Solomon couldn't avoid this reality: God is uncontainable. However great a dwelling-place he built, how could it be majestic enough for the God of creation? And yet, amazingly, the God who had dwelt in the "thick darkness" of Mount Sinai did come and did

---

21 2 Chronicles 2:5.

meet with His people there.[22] It's virtually impossible to read the opening chapters of 2 Chronicles without being struck—as Solomon was—by the fact that the Creator God had once again condescended to dwell with His people, in yet another picture of God's desire for redemption and relationship.

Yet as special as the temple was as the place where God met with His people, there remained a sense that the plan was as yet incomplete. Why was this? Because God's plan was always centered on a person and not an object or a place.

As you read your Bible, that truth comes up again and again. Think about the woman at the well in John 4. The woman comes to fill her pots with water, and in the course of her conversation with Jesus, she asks a "place" question: "How is it that you, a Jew, ask for a drink from me, a woman of Samaria … Our fathers worshiped on this mountain, but you say that in Jerusalem is the place where people ought to worship."[23] But to paraphrase Jesus, He essentially says, *It's not about a place; it's about a person. Those who truly worship the Father do so in spirit and truth, and I am the one sent to make that possible.*[24]

Jesus Himself is God's eternal Word at work; the one who was "in the beginning" could not be fully contained in Solomon's temple, yet He chose to take on human

---

22 2 Chronicles 6:1; 7:1-2.
23 John 4:9, 20.
24 John 4:22-26.

form. Why? To dwell among us for a little while so that we might dwell with Him forever. Instead of saying, "Did God dwell on earth?" our knowledge of the New Testament allows us to flip the first two words and say, "God *did* dwell on earth."

J.I. Packer put it this way: "Nothing in fiction is so fantastic as is this truth of the incarnation."[25] It is a staggering thought, isn't it? The God of eternity appeared in the person of the Son to live in His own creation without ceasing to be God. The fullness of God was contained in a human body. He who fashioned the cosmos became a speck in His own cosmos. He dwelt with His people in the wilderness, in the temple, and in human frailty.

And He still dwells with His people today.

Most of us spend (or at least aim to spend) a good portion of each Christmas season reflecting on the fact that God dwelt among us in the person of our Lord Jesus. But having lived, died, and risen again, Jesus is now physically present at the right hand of the Father on high. How, then, does God now dwell on earth, in time and space? The answer is found in the one whom Jesus promised to have His Father send:

> *I will ask the Father, and he will give you*
> *another Helper, to be with you forever, even the*

---

25 J.I. Packer, *Knowing God* (InterVarsity Press, 2021), p 53.

Spirit of truth, whom the world cannot receive,
because it neither sees him nor knows him. You
know him, for he dwells with you and will be in
you. (John 14:16-17)

God has graciously poured His Holy Spirit into those
for whom His Son came and lived and died and rose.
Those who have trusted in Him, those who love Him,
those who have been assembled as living stones, gathered to Christ our cornerstone, are now the very place
where God dwells.

This Christmas, we can stand amazed—just as Solomon did at the temple dedication—as we consider the
fact that God did indeed dwell on earth. And remember, if you are in Christ, "*you* also are being built together into a dwelling place for God by the Spirit," and
"God's temple is holy, and *you* are that temple."[26] God
has built His own house in which to dwell on earth: His
church—you and me.

For Reflection:
What difference to your view of yourself and of your
church does today's reading make?

---

26 Ephesians 2:22; 1 Corinthians 3:17.

Our God, heaven cannot hold Him,
Nor earth sustain;
Heaven and earth shall flee away
When He comes to reign:
In the bleak midwinter
A stable place sufficed
The Lord God Almighty,
Jesus Christ.

What can I give Him,
Poor as I am?
If I were a shepherd,
I would bring a lamb,
If I were a wise man
I would do my part,
Yet what I can I give Him,
Give my heart.

"In the Bleak Midwinter"
Christina Rossetti

7. A LIGHT HAS DAWNED

"The people who walked in darkness
have seen a great light; those who dwelt in a land of
deep darkness, on them has light shone."
ISAIAH 9:2

The Bible never disguises just how dark life can get.
The Scriptures are clear that when God is left out—
when we choose our way over His—darkness results.

The days in which the prophet Isaiah lived were dark
indeed. Solomon's great temple was the site not of real
worship but of self-serving corruption. Wicked kings
failed to point Israel back to their true King. Injustice
reigned. God's people had grown used to ignoring His
prophets. And yet life did not work out for them. The
darkness of their own hearts and conduct was matched
by the looming darkness of invasion from the north,
from the mighty Assyrians.

All this left them "greatly distressed and hungry," but
such was their rejection of the Lord that they chose
to "speak contemptuously against their king and their
God." It would have been reasonable for the Lord to
have left them to experience the "distress and darkness,

the gloom of anguish," without hope or future.[27] They didn't want Him. He would only have been giving them what they had chosen.

But our God is a promise-keeping God.

Isaiah 9 begins with a glorious reversal. Just where we might anticipate reading that God will turn His face away from these rebellious people, we read, "There will be no more gloom for her who was in anguish."[28] The Lord would not leave His people, and He would not allow them to remain in misery. No, for these people in darkness, "on them has light shone." God's light would break into the self-inflicted gloom of sin, ultimately and supremely in the form of the promised Messiah.

Isaiah was writing about 800 years before Jesus, though, so why was he writing about Christ's advent as if it had already happened? Answer: because it was so vivid, so clear, and so certain in his mind that, under the inspiration of the Holy Spirit, he could use the prophetic perfect tense in order to make clear exactly what was going to take place. That's why Peter, when he wrote about the prophets from the vantage point of the first century, on the other side of the coming of Christ, said that the prophets were, in a sense, standing on tiptoe, looking to see the fulfillment of the things that they had written.[29]

---

27 Isaiah 8:21-22.
28 Isaiah 9:1.
29 1 Peter 1:10-11.

But *how*? How could Isaiah's prophecy come about? How can darkness be replaced by light, war be replaced by peace, distress be replaced by joy? "*You*," writes the prophet, "have multiplied the nation; *you* have increased its joy."[30] Who is it that has caused all this to take place? Answer: God alone, for He is the source of light, and it is in His light alone that we truly see. There is no way for the sorrowful to be comforted, for the broken to be healed, for this light to dawn upon a human heart and mind—except that God does it.

Just when it appears as though the wintertime of the soul is about to come in all of its crushing sadness, God's light shines. And it is a dazzling light, because He is the God of immeasurable mercy and grace. He enters into the darkness and emptiness of our experiences to bring His light, His joy, and His peace. It's a story which is so wonderfully conveyed to us in the celebration of lights that we enjoy at this time of year.

Not long after Isaiah had come and gone, the people of God again found themselves in anguish. Foreign rulers had triumphed over them, and no prophetic word had been heard for many, many years. *Perhaps He's really done it this time,* the people may have thought. *Maybe the Lord has finally had enough.*

---

30 Isaiah 9:3.

But we know better. We know that into this darkness a child was born. The good news of Christmas is that the God of the Bible, the Light of the world, came down and entered the darkness, and it could not overcome Him. Are you walking in darkness today, whether that is the darkness of your own sin or the darkness caused by the sin of others? Remember, God is neither afraid of nor defeated by these things. Be encouraged, for in Jesus, God has drawn near. By His Spirit, He can and will bring light to the dark. Look to Him and walk in His light.

For Reflection:
Reread the previous paragraph. Does your perspective on this world, or your own circumstances, need to change? What difference will the light make to you today?

> *O come, O come, Emmanuel,*
> *And ransom captive Israel,*
> *That mourns in lonely exile here*
> *Until the Son of God appear.*
> *Rejoice! Rejoice! Emmanuel*
> *Shall come to you, O Israel.*
>
> *O come, O Wisdom from on high,*
> *Who ordered all things mightily;*
> *To us the path of knowledge show*
> *And teach us in its ways to go.*
> *Rejoice! Rejoice! Emmanuel*
> *Shall come to you, O Israel.*

O come, O Bright and Morning Star,
And bring us comfort from afar!
Dispel the shadows of the night
And turn our darkness into light.
Rejoice! Rejoice! Emmanuel
Shall come to you, O Israel.

O come, O King of nations, bind
In one the hearts of all mankind.
Bid all our sad divisions cease
And be Yourself our King of Peace.
Rejoice! Rejoice! Emmanuel
Shall come to you, O Israel.

"O Come, O Come, Emmanuel"
Latin hymn, trans. by John M. Neale

8. TO US A CHILD IS BORN

"For to us a child is born, to us a son is given; and the
government shall be upon his shoulder, and his name
shall be called Wonderful Counselor, Mighty God,
Everlasting Father, Prince of Peace."

ISAIAH 9:6

Christmas is God's definitive answer to all of the
world's darkness and all of life's disappointments.
At Christmas, the answer to the hopes and fears of all
the years is found in a single newborn baby.

Godly men and women had been looking for
the birth of this child ever since the promise of a
serpent-crusher in Eden. The people of Israel had long
been awaiting the arrival of the one who would embody
all of their hopes. The prophets had been declaring the
coming of a Messiah, and the expectation of such a deliverer steadily grew. And, as he prophesied the coming
of light to the darkness, Isaiah added significant fuel
to the fire of this longing by giving wonderful detail
about the identity and work of this coming King. In
Isaiah's day, the people of God still had centuries to
wait before His arrival. But we do not. Today, peer

with me into that first-century food trough and marvel at the one who lay there.

———

This child is our "Wonderful Counselor." In the ancient world, kings were known in some measure by their counselors. The extent of their authority and rule was made apparent by the number of advisers they could call upon for guidance. A wise ruler is honest enough to recognize they cannot possibly know everything about everything, and therefore they need people to give them advice. And yet this King, Isaiah said, would have none—not because He lacks wisdom but because He is the embodiment of it. He Himself is the Wonderful Counselor; He has no need of any outside wisdom in order to rule with absolute perfection as well as total authority. He requires no advice, He makes no mistakes, and He never merely guesses as to the best way forward, for Himself or His subjects. As a Wonderful Counselor, He has a perfect plan.

———

This child is our "Mighty God." And therefore He has the power to execute that perfect plan. After all, a plan in and of itself is no good if you cannot execute it. But here is a king who can walk on water, and heal the sick, and raise the dead. He is the divine King, and nothing is too hard for Him. Christ's authority will never come to an end, for He is the Lord of creation. The wonder of wonders, miracle of miracles, is that this God has entered into our circumstances, assumed the frailty of the creatures, and embraced human weakness in the fullness of His power. Never let it cease to amaze you that as with the eyes of faith you peer into that food trough at the baby who lies inside, you are looking at the Mighty God.

This child is our "Everlasting Father." Here, we move from God's plan and His power to His paternity. The child who was promised in Isaiah is our Everlasting Father. This title here is not a reference to the first Person of the Trinity, for it was God the Son who took on human flesh. Isaiah is saying that Jesus is like a perfect father to His people:

> *Fatherlike He tends and spares us;*
> *Well our feeble frame He knows.*
> *In His hand He gently bears us,*
> *Rescues us from all our foes.*[31]

In other words, having brought us into His family, Jesus will forever hold us fast. He hasn't gone to the extent of seeking us out, forgiving us, embracing us, and drawing us to Himself in order that He might just cast us aside. "Everlasting" is not merely a reference to His eternal being; it is a reference to the never-ending dimension of His care. There will never be a day when the Lord Jesus

---

31 Henry Francis Lyte, "Praise, My Soul, the King of Heaven" (1834).

does not know what you need. There will never be a day when the Lord Jesus is not able to do what you need. And there will never be a day when the Lord Jesus does not long to do what you need, for His love for you is father-like. There is no limit to, and can be no end to, His love for you. The Lord of creation tends to us each day, in every way, like a perfect father.

⸺

This child is our "Prince of Peace." Sin spoils things for all of us. It separates us from one another and from God. All of us by nature are "alienated and hostile in mind" to our Creator.[32] But the Prince of Peace has come! Jesus Christ can end the conflict between God and humanity, for He crossed the divide between God and us in His incarnation, and He bridged the divide between us and God in His death and resurrection. He is the only one who is able to take the place that we deserve to take because of our sin; He is the only one who loves us enough to choose to take our place, despite our sin. Finding true peace and prosperity is not about personal achievement. It is not about us fixing ourselves or being better people next year than we were this year. It's about embracing what Christ has achieved.

⸺

Our Wonderful Counselor, Mighty God, Everlasting Father, and Prince of Peace has come. Without Jesus,

---

32 Colossians 1:21.

if we possess everything, we really have nothing; and with Jesus, even if we possess nothing, we really have everything. We can joyfully submit to His plans, bow the knee to His rule, rely on His tender care, and let His peace dwell in our hearts. For to us this child, this King, has been born.

For Reflection:
Which of the four descriptions of the Lord Jesus that we have enjoyed today did you particularly appreciate? What does it prompt you to praise Jesus for, and what does it lead you to ask Him to do in or for you?

> *It came upon the midnight clear,*
> *That glorious song of old,*
> *From angels bending near the earth*
> *To touch their harps of gold:*
> *"Peace on the earth, good will to men,*
> *From heaven's all-gracious King."*
> *The world in solemn stillness lay*
> *To hear the angels sing.*
>
> *And ye, beneath life's crushing load,*
> *Whose forms are bending low,*
> *Who toil along the climbing way*
> *With painful steps and slow,*
> *Look now! For glad and golden hours*
> *Come swiftly on the wing.*
> *O rest beside the weary road*
> *And hear the angels sing!*

For lo! The days are hastening on
By prophet seen of old,
When with the ever-circling years
Shall come the time foretold.
When peace shall over all the earth
Its ancient splendors fling,
And the whole world send back the song
Which now the angels sing.

"It Came Upon the Midnight Clear"
Edmund H. Sears

9. TIDINGS OF COMFORT AND JOY

"Comfort, comfort my people, says your God ... A voice cries: 'In the wilderness prepare the way of the LORD; make straight in the desert a highway for our God ... Every valley shall be lifted up, and every mountain and hill be made low; the uneven ground shall become level, and the rough places a plain. And the glory of the LORD shall be revealed, and all flesh shall see it together, for the mouth of the LORD has spoken.'"

ISAIAH 40:1, 3-5

"God Rest Ye Merry, Gentlemen" is a traditional English carol that has been around for a long time now. In Charles Dickens's novella *A Christmas Carol*, this carol makes an early but interrupted appearance. A caroler begins singing the first lines, but "at the first sound ... Scrooge seized the ruler with such energy of action that the singer fled in terror."[33] Scrooge was

---

33 Charles Dickens, *A Christmas Carol* (1843), stave 1.

a stranger to the "tidings of comfort and joy" that the chorus announces.

Long before this story was written by Dickens, long before the carol was first sung, a very straightforward message was given by God to His messengers: "Comfort, comfort my people." This message was extended to those who were in the doldrums—isolated, oppressed, despondent. And (though they did not wish to accept it) the reason why they found themselves in such a position was essentially that they had stopped listening to God and to His servants. Instead of obeying Him, they had decided that they would try to figure out life on their own; instead of acknowledging Him, they had ignored Him. And then they had concluded that God had forgotten them: that He did not care about them.

But the truth was the other way around. The people might wander from God, but God would never give up on His people. What a comfort!

⸺⸺

This message of comfort from Isaiah can be helpfully summarized with four words. The first is *proclamation*. It is true to say that Isaiah uttered these words, but it is equally true to say that "the mouth of the LORD has spoken." What we have is a strange duality and the wonderful reality that God is the ultimate messenger, choosing to convey His message through human instruments. And His message is one of comfort.

What is this comfort that is being proclaimed? "Warfare is ended … iniquity is pardoned," and the wages of sin have been paid.[34] God is essentially saying to His people, *This failure, this disobedience, has gone on long enough.* The people had sinned, and they had suffered for it, but that was not the end of their story.

Isaiah 40 is a prophetic word—one that was spoken into the realities of Isaiah's own day but that also had a future reality yet to unfold in all its fullness. Even still, it speaks to us today. We have sinned, and we have suffered for it, and the world is full of the consequences of humanity's rebellion against our Creator. But—as Isaiah reminds us again and again—that is not the end of our story. God graciously comforts His chosen people: "I am he who blots out your transgressions for my own sake, and I will not remember your sins," He tells us. "I have blotted out your transgressions like a cloud and your sins like mist; return to me, for I have redeemed you."[35] One was coming to bear sins and carry sorrows[36]: one who, in Himself, would hold out comfort and joy.

The task, then, is one of *preparation*—our second word. A key part of the messengers' proclamation is to cry out, "prepare the way of the LORD." So it was that John the Baptist was given the ministry of announcing the coming of the Lord Jesus. He was the fulfillment of Isaiah 40:3. But there is a certain respect in which we are all in the line of John the Baptist.

---

34 Isaiah 40:2.
35 Isaiah 43:25; 44:22.
36 Isaiah 53:4-6.

How will our friends, neighbors, and loved ones know that Jesus has come to bring comfort and joy? By hearing the message of the gospel. How can they be invited to prepare the way for His second advent, to stand ready to receive Him? From our lips. Christians are messengers, whoever we are and wherever God has set us. The significance of our task is not found in who we are but in the wonder of this message which we have been given to proclaim: *Prepare to meet the God against whom you have sinned, but who has come to make an end of all your sin and suffering.*

That brings us to verse 4 and our third word: *transformation*. When we read that uneven terrain will "become level," God is saying that when He comes, He's going to deal with the obstacles—unbelief, temptation, injustice, and more. So much stands between this world as it is and the world that God has promised it will one day be—much of it, indeed, within our own hearts. What can you and I do about all that? In one sense the answer is: nothing! But that's a comfort, not a discouragement. For only God is able to break down walls. Only God can raise valleys, flatten mountains, and renew a heart of stone. And He promises to be about that work.

What are your struggles? Are you finding yourself unable to deal with the heights of pride, the depths of lack of self-esteem, or the length of your trials? Remember, God will get you to the level ground. God can take you through and over what you could never scale alone.

He never actually suffers setbacks. He overcomes all the hindrances. He travels without difficulty, He always arrives without fail, and He's always on time.

<hr>

This leads us to our final word: *revelation*. "The glory of the LORD shall be revealed, and all flesh shall see it together." God's glory is His character: who He is. God's glory is that He is merciful, gracious, holy, abounding in love, slow to anger, faithful to His covenant promises, and so much more.[37] And He has revealed this glory, most fully and wonderfully, as "the Word became flesh and dwelt among us, and we have seen his glory, glory as of the only Son from the Father, full of grace and truth."[38] Isaiah was looking forward to Christmas. All that may be known of God in human form is found in Jesus, and that is why His advent is worthy of such deep reflection and great celebration.

<hr>

Here, then, is true comfort and real joy. God has spoken. Sin and suffering are not the end of the story. The conclusion relies on God's work, and not ours. Here is hope for the weariest heart and warmth for the coldest. Here is what saves us from becoming Scrooges ourselves, even as we deal with the challenges and difficulties of life. God has broken into history, we have seen His glory,

---

37 Exodus 34:6.
38 John 1:14.

and this is where we find our greatest and our unshakable tidings of comfort and joy.

For Reflection:
How do these truths bring you, in your particular circumstances, comfort and joy? And who do you know with whom you can share this message, pointing them toward the source of true comfort and joy for them, too?

> *God rest ye merry, gentlemen,*
> *Let nothing you dismay.*
> *Remember Christ our Savior*
> *Was born on Christmas Day*
> *To save us all from Satan's pow'r*
> *When we were gone astray.*
> *O tidings of comfort and joy,*
> *Comfort and joy,*
> *O tidings of comfort and joy.*
>
> *From God our heav'nly Father*
> *A blessed angel came*
> *And unto certain shepherds*
> *Brought tidings of the same:*
> *How that in Bethlehem was born*
> *The Son of God by name.*
> *O tidings of comfort and joy,*
> *Comfort and joy,*
> *O tidings of comfort and joy.*
>
> *"God Rest Ye Merry, Gentlemen"*
> *An English carol*

10. O LITTLE TOWN
OF BETHLEHEM

*"But you, O Bethlehem Ephrathah, who are too little
to be among the clans of Judah, from you shall come
forth for me one who is to be ruler in Israel, whose
coming forth is from of old, from ancient days …
And he shall stand and shepherd his flock in the
strength of the LORD, in the majesty of the name of
the LORD his God. And they shall dwell secure, for
now he shall be great to the ends of the earth. And he
shall be their peace."*

MICAH 5:2, 4-5

Seventy years ago, the pastor and Bible translator J.B.
Phillips delivered a series of lectures that later became a book. In one address, he made this observation:

*"We face to-day a world torn and divided.
So widespread is the distress of nations, so
complex the problems which face every thinking
Christian, that I think we may be forgiven if
our hearts sometimes fail us … But for our*

*comfort we may fairly remind ourselves that
the worldwide tensions and sufferings only seem
to us to be more overwhelming than they did
to our forefathers because we are much better
informed about them through modern means of
news-transmission than they could ever be."* [39]

Phillips was referring to technology like newsreel radio broadcasts. Can you imagine what he would make of things like social media, smartphones, and 24-hour news channels? It's never been easier to stay informed. In some ways, that is a blessing; in other ways, it is over-whelming and anxiety-inducing. Each technological breakthrough comes with the promise that it will bring people together—and yet, in every generation, people still find peace elusive, even as they long for it.

Micah's generation was no different. The people yearned for peace. Nearly seven centuries before Christ's first advent, foreigners had besieged Jerusalem, and the city's people could barely lift a finger in their own defense. They were a subjugated people, unable to gather enough troops together to fight back against the enemy. Theirs was a picture of absolute disgrace.

It must have been a very confusing time for God's people. They were supposed to be a chosen people, set apart for God, the carriers of His great promise to bless

39 J.B. Phillips, *Making Men Whole* (Wipf & Stock Publishers, 2012), p 13.

74

and restore the world, but now it appeared that all of that was about to be destroyed. They likely would have thought to themselves, *Where are God's promises? Will we ever again find peace?*

The answer wasn't what they expected.

Hope was coming, Micah announced; but the surprise was where that hope was coming from. The promised ruler, who would reverse the defeats, heal the divisions, and bring peace, would come not from Jerusalem but from Bethlehem.

Jerusalem was the royal city, the location of the temple, and the primary geographic focus of God's people. Bethlehem, on the other hand, would not have been on anyone's radar. It was "too little to be among the clans of Judah." It wouldn't have made their Top 100 list, let alone the Top 10. Yet the significance of Bethlehem is found in its insignificance.

Thinking about the rest of the Bible story, we realize that this makes perfect sense. This is how God works! When Goliath taunted the people of Israel, the strong and brave soldiers of Israel fled. Instead, God used a small, insignificant shepherd boy—from Bethlehem, of all places!—with five stones and a sling to deliver God's people. This is God's way.

Now, Micah announced, once more a Shepherd-King would come from the little town of Bethlehem. He would stand in the place of authority, shepherd His flock in the strength of Yahweh, and grant security to those who trust in Him. In Him, Micah said, God's people would finally find lasting peace.

This is not a message that anyone who wants to be accepted and believed by the masses would ever invent! Yet it was into this insignificant place that the Messiah came to rule. The one who lay in a Bethlehem food trough was the one with a never-ending kingdom which surpasses all other kingdoms. The birth of the one through whom all things were made was announced to a few insignificant shepherds instead of the cultural elites.

Recognizing the pattern of God's ways in ancient days enables us to recognize that this is exactly the kind of thing we should expect at the first Christmas, for this is how God works: in the quiet places, in the forgotten places, and through those who are weak and unimpressive. It readies us for the reality that the one upon whom all God's promises rested would die a humiliating death on a cross. It reminds us that this is God's way and always has been. And it changes the way we look at our own lives.

⸻

I have a little booklet called *Five Minutes' Peace*.[40] It tells the story of a mother elephant who just wants five minutes of peace away from her children—but as soon as she attempts to get peace, more chaos ensues. This is surely something that every mother can identify with! In the midst of chaos, we long for a few moments of respite, but it frequently seems unattainable. Look around

---

40 Jill Murphy, *Five Minutes' Peace* (Walker, 1986).

you and you'll see that true peace appears to be virtually absent globally, nationally, locally, and personally. Even just five minutes' peace is beyond us and our world—let alone lasting peace.

Is your life this Christmas marked in one way or another by fractured relationships, financial distress, personal loss, or other disappointments? If so, here is good news for you: in Jesus, the Messiah who was born in the little town of Bethlehem, you will find genuine, lasting peace. This peace is first and foremost with God Himself, and then it is with ourselves and within our relationships and communities, as we learn to reflect the God of peace in the way we approach tensions, difficulties, and conflicts.

God is at work, often in ways unseen by most and unreported in the scrolling media channels—just as in Micah's day and just as in Jesus' day. But this is a world into which the Messiah, the Prince of Peace, has come to bring this supernatural and eternal peace to all who trust in Him. Whatever else you face, you can enjoy the peace with your Creator that He died to win for you. Then, knowing you are at peace with the only one whose opinion matters eternally, you will be able to walk out into your world to seek, by His grace, to live at peace.

For Reflection:

Is there a relationship that you can seek to bring peace to today, empowered by knowing you are already at peace with God?

Does the truth that God works in the quiet and forgotten places, through those who are weak and unimpressive, need to humble you a little or raise you up a little?

> *O little town of Bethlehem,*
> *How still we see thee lie!*
> *Above thy deep and dreamless sleep,*
> *The silent stars go by.*
> *Yet in thy dark streets shineth*
> *The everlasting light;*
> *The hopes and fears of all the years*
> *Are met in thee tonight.*
>
> *For Christ is born of Mary;*
> *And, gathered all above,*
> *While mortals sleep, the angels keep*
> *Their watch of wond'ring love.*
> *O morning stars, together*
> *Proclaim the holy birth,*
> *And praises sing to God the King,*
> *And peace to men on earth.*
>
> *How silently, how silently,*
> *The wondrous gift is giv'n!*
> *So God imparts to human hearts*
> *The blessings of His heav'n.*
> *No ear may hear His coming,*

But in this world of sin,
Where meek souls will receive Him still,
The dear Christ enters in.

O holy Child of Bethlehem,
Descend to us, we pray;
Cast out our sin and enter in;
Be born in us today.
We hear the Christmas angels
The great glad tidings tell;
O come to us, abide with us,
Our Lord Emmanuel!

"O Little Town of Bethlehem"
Phillips Brooks

PART 3

CHRISTMAS
IN THE GOSPELS

.

II. EVERY PROMISE KEPT

*"The book of the genealogy of Jesus Christ, the son of
David, the son of Abraham."*
MATTHEW 1:1

The beginning of the New Testament may not immediately strike us as very inspiring! In fact, if
someone were reading through the Bible for the very
first time and reached the end of the Old Testament
and the book of Malachi, which points forward with
anticipation, their excitement might falter when the
next book begins with… a genealogy. They (and we!)
might be tempted to skip Matthew and begin with another Gospel altogether.

In fact, it hit me a few years ago that I spent more
than three decades of ministry skipping over the first
17 verses of this Gospel during Christmastime. I would
head straight for verse 18: "Now the birth of Jesus Christ
took place in this way…" Realizing I had done this year
after year prompted me to consider more carefully the
great list of names that Matthew's genealogy contains.

Mark gets right to business, Luke provides a clari-
fication of his approach and a dedication to his first

reader, and John begins in a beautifully poetic manner as he reflects on the deity and eternality of Jesus. Why does Matthew begin with a list? Because he wants to make clear that we cannot understand Jesus' arrival unless we understand it in light of the big picture that the Bible provides—unless we see it in the grand scheme of God's unfolding plans and purposes. (Matthew, I think, would have approved of our approach to this Advent devotional, starting in Genesis and reaching his Gospel only on Day 11!)

The first-century Jewish readers of Matthew's Gospel were waiting to see how God would fulfill His promises through His Messiah. And that is why, in fact, the New Testament couldn't open in a more fitting manner, since the genealogy in Matthew draws the line from Abraham to David and all the way through to Jesus the Messiah, the one who fulfills all the promises God made to His people through the centuries. Matthew is telling the amazing story of God's faithfulness in blessing all the nations on the earth, as He had promised Abraham; he is unpacking the royal line to demonstrate how God stayed true to His covenant with King David by sending King Jesus; he is showing that the time of spiritual exile was drawing to a close, just as the physical exile had done. The value of this long list is in recognizing the roles of these individuals in God's unfolding plan, which culminates in the birth of Jesus. And it is in recognizing that the line goes through difficulties and dark times—through the valleys as well as over the mountaintops—and yet God was working out His purposes day by day and generation by generation. The thread from Abraham through David to Christ Jesus may have looked thin, but God ensured it was never broken.

In a similar fashion, Mark, throughout his Gospel, reaches one hand back to the prophets who pointed forward to the one who was yet to come. "As it is written in Isaiah the prophet…", Mark says in his second sentence.[41] And (having skipped the events of the first Christmas) the first appearance of Jesus that Mark records is of Him as an adult, and the first words Jesus says in Mark's Gospel are "The time is fulfilled, and the kingdom of God is at hand."[42] Jesus' disciples had the privilege of witnessing what prophets and kings had longed to see—a privilege that even now continues through the illuminating work of God's word.

The New Testament shows us that the means by which God's promises are fulfilled, and the entirety of the plan God worked out through the Old Testament age, can be summed up in two words: *Jesus Christ*. God made His promises to Israel using terminology and categories that they understood—words like "nation" and "temple." Christ's coming redefined Old Testament concepts in light of the gospel: Old Testament prophecies, we discover, are all fulfilled christologically—by and in the person of the Christ. Therefore, for example, instead

---

41 Mark 1:2.
42 Mark 1:15.

of looking for a new temple in the state of Israel, we meet with God through His Son, the Lord Jesus; we enjoy His presence in each of us by His Spirit; and we look to the reality of Christ's reign to transform our lives both now and forevermore. The coming of the Son of God breaks the boundaries of Old Testament categories. Christ is the perfect fulfillment of all God's promises, and He is the reality of all God's great assurances.

So we wait no more to see how God will fulfill His every promise. We know now that each one was, is, and ever will be satisfied through Christ. He has promised to be with us, to work for us and through us, and to bring us to an eternal kingdom of perfection. There are times when it is hard to hold onto those promises. When those times come, we look up to the God who is always at work, in the darker valleys of our lives as well as on the sunnier hilltops, and we trust that though we may not see it now, we will one day appreciate how He was working for our good and His glory. And we look back to a man born of Abraham's and David's line, conceived of the Spirit, who was able to announce that the time of fulfillment had come and that the kingdom of God was at hand, and who hung on the cross and rose from the grave to make it so.

For Reflection:
Which of God's promises do you find hardest to believe He is keeping or will keep? How can the events of the first Christmas give you deeper confidence that you can trust God to keep those promises?

For unto us a Child is born,
Unto us a Son is given,
And the government shall be upon His
shoulder:
And His name shall be called
Wonderful, Counselor,
The Mighty God,
The Everlasting Father,
The Prince of Peace.

"For Unto Us a Child Is Born"
The Messiah: Part I, Movement 12
George Frederick Handel

12. WONDER AND MYSTERY

"'Behold, you will conceive in your womb and bear a son, and you shall call his name Jesus' … And Mary said to the angel, 'How will this be, since I am a virgin?' And the angel answered her, 'The Holy Spirit will come upon you, and the power of the Most High will overshadow you; therefore the child to be born will be called holy—the Son of God.'"

LUKE 1:31, 34-35

It is not the circumstances of Jesus' *birth* which are most remarkable but rather those of His *conception*. When the angel announced that although she was a virgin, Mary would have a baby who would rule the entire universe, she simply asked the sensible question, "How?" And with that question, we arrive at the very heart of the Christmas story—and the Christian's story.

How was this child to be conceived? God was going to make it happen. He would do it. The language of being overshadowed is resonant of God's divine presence being symbolized to the Israelites by a great cloud.[43] The conception, in other words, would be supernatural—able to be accomplished by God alone. And the one to be born was Himself supernatural—the holy Son of God.

The early Christians studied the Scriptures carefully as they hammered out the incarnation's implications in order to describe faithfully and truthfully the one who was conceived by the Spirit in Mary's womb. And so they came to the wording that has passed down to us in the early creeds. Our spiritual forefathers identified the wonder of the incarnation, bowed before the mystery of it, and affirmed that Jesus was, and remains, very God and very man. Their encapsulation of the mystery of the incarnation is well worth reflecting on and delighting in:

> *We believe in ... one Lord Jesus Christ,*
> *the only Son of God,*
> *begotten from the Father before all ages,*
> *God from God,*
> *Light from Light,*
> *true God from true God,*
> *begotten, not made;*
> *of the same essence as the Father.*
> *Through Him all things were made.*
> *For us and for our salvation*
> *He came down from heaven;*
> *He became incarnate by the Holy Spirit*

---

43 Exodus 40:34-38.

and the virgin Mary,
and was made human. (Nicene Creed, AD 325)

Each Christmas, we face the temptation to allow familiarity with the Nativity scene to breed complacency and to blind us to the awe-inspiring truth that as we look at the baby in a Bethlehem manger, we are looking in on God Himself in the form of a servant.

This Servant had a mission. He came "for us and for our salvation." He came "to open the eyes that are blind, to bring out the prisoners from the dungeon, from the prison those who sit in darkness."[44]

During Jesus' earthly ministry, He gave a wonderful illustration of this by granting healing to the physically blind. The greatest need, however, was not physical sight but spiritual sight. He came to open the eyes of men and women who were blind to God's truth.

The God-Man also came to free captives from their bondage. Many of us have felt the captivity of our guilt, trying countless hoped-for solutions to resist our sin and escape from its consequences. But nothing works except Jesus. He breaks our chains and sets us free. Once slaves of sin, we have now been rescued. Our Savior releases from the dungeon those who sit in darkness, if only they see His light.

The story of the Servant is a story not about what we must do but about what Jesus has done. He came down into the darkness, came down into our enslavement,

---

44 Isaiah 42:7.

came down into our blindness, and said, *You've failed and broken the law, and you are entirely unable to rectify your condition. But I save sinners. I open blind eyes. I release captives. I bring light. I have done everything required for you. Turn to Me in simple faith and childlike trust, and you will see. You will be free, and your darkness will give way to sunshine.*

⟡

The first Christmas declares that God supernaturally intervenes in the affairs of this world to bring about His good purposes. The conversion of every Christian declares the same great truth. It takes a supernatural invasion of God into individuals' lives to bring them to saving faith, just as God sovereignly worked a miracle in Mary's womb in order to bring us the Savior. Jesus told Nicodemus, the religious leader, that unless someone is born from above—a birth brought about by God through the Holy Spirit—they would not see God's kingdom.[45] If we have been brought to salvation, it is only because God has done it. We did no more to free ourselves from the captivity of sin than Mary did to become pregnant with our Savior. The "How?" of salvation is always answered only by "God did it."

So, bow today before the wonder and mystery of God taking on flesh. And bow today before the wonder and mystery of God opening your eyes to your need of His Son as your Savior. For that story, no less than the

---

45 John 3:3.

conception of the Son of God in a virgin's womb, is the supernatural work of God.

For Reflection:

Reflect on your own conversion to faith in Christ. How does it prompt you to worship and thank God? And how does it prompt you to share Christ with those around you?

> *What Child is this, who, laid to rest,*
> *On Mary's lap is sleeping,*
> *Whom angels greet with anthems sweet,*
> *While shepherds watch are keeping?*
> *This, this is Christ, the King,*
> *Whom shepherds guard and angels sing:*
> *Haste, haste to bring Him laud,*
> *The Babe, the Son of Mary!*
>
> *Why lies He in such mean estate,*
> *Where ox and ass are feeding?*
> *Good Christian, fear: for sinners here,*
> *The silent Word is pleading.*
> *This, this is Christ, the King,*
> *Whom shepherds guard and angels sing:*
> *Haste, haste to bring Him laud,*
> *The Babe, the Son of Mary!*
>
> *So bring Him incense, gold, and myrrh,*
> *Come, peasant, king to own Him.*
> *The King of kings salvation brings;*
> *Let loving hearts enthrone Him.*

This, this is Christ, the King,
Whom shepherds guard and angels sing:
Haste, haste to bring Him laud,
The Babe, the Son of Mary!

"What Child Is This?"
William Chatterton Dix

13. HOW SWEET THE NAME

"Joseph, son of David, do not fear to take Mary as your
wife, for that which is conceived in her is from the
Holy Spirit. She will bear a son, and you shall call his
name Jesus, for he will save his people from their sins."

MATTHEW 1:20-21

The child at the heart of the first Christmas has many
glorious names: King, Creator, Lord, Judge, Son of
God, Son of David, Master, the I Am, the First and the
Last, and so on. But the angel commanded Joseph that a
very specific name be given to Him at His birth—and it
is worth asking what God's intention behind that choice
was. Why "Jesus"?

The name itself was not an unusual name. It is the
Greek version of the Old Testament Hebrew name
Joshua, or *Yeshua*, and simply translated it means "The
Lord saves." So of all the glorious names He might have
been given, the name that would mark out the incarnate Son of God would be a consistent reminder that
in Him, God is doing a saving work. He was to be so
named, said the angel, "for he will save his people from
their sins." As Peter would later proclaim, "There is no

other name under heaven given among men by which we must be saved."[46]

This is a precious name, yet so many treat it as peripheral or even profane. Many people have no interest in the name "Jesus," except perhaps as a curse word. Many feel that their lives are too busy to think about the implications of His name for them, and so Jesus is ultimately sidelined. Still others are lost in their desire to have an open mind: to embrace any and every view of the divine as valid. But in the process, their open minds have closed their hearts to belief in the God who really came from heaven to save people on earth. They believe He may be an example and an advisor and an inspiration, but He cannot be the way in which the real Son of God came to save real people from their real sins. This may sound honoring, but it denies the very meaning of Jesus' name.

It is easy for those of us who own the name of Christians—the kind of people who read a devotional during Advent—to shake our heads at all that. But we ought to challenge ourselves, too, for professing Christians are not immune from the danger of profaning the name of Jesus. Pious religious routines that lack the substance of faith in the risen Lord undermine the reality of which His name speaks. To call ourselves Christians if our lives have not been changed and we have no intimate awareness of Jesus is to take His name in vain.[47] To be

---

46 Acts 4:12.

47 Exodus 20:7.

a Christian is not simply to perform the good works and religious ceremonies that the Bible prescribes and to avoid the deeds that the Bible proscribes. It is, rather, to be united to Christ by grace through faith—to know Him and to trust Him.

⌐————⌐

Perhaps this Christmas season, then, provides a helpful moment to pause and to ask ourselves honestly, "What does the name Jesus mean to me?" If you have been brought face to face with your sin and have come to believe that Jesus is your Savior, no name will be more precious to you than His. There may have been a time when you might have held Him at arm's length or thought that you could save yourself through good works, but not now. Now the name, the person, and the work of Jesus are dear to you, for you have drawn near to Him and experienced His compassion, kindness, and mercy.

Jesus will either be everything to us this Christmas or He will be nothing. But if we know Him as our Savior, then how sweet His name sounds to us! Here is the name that assures us of our forgiveness and our future; that comforts us in our losses and frailties; that gives us joy in the ups and downs of daily life; that stills our soul when troubles come:

How sweet the name of Jesus sounds
In a believer's ear!
It soothes our sorrows, heals our wounds,
And drives away our fear.[48]

Yes, Jesus was born in a manger in Bethlehem so that He could, as the angel told Joseph, "save his people from their sins," restoring them to peace with God and giving them the promise of eternal life with Him. The name given to the incarnate Son of God was significant. Before you put this book down to move along with your day or go to sleep, why not take a few minutes simply to reflect on the name "Jesus"—to consider just how precious that name is to you and to rest in the assurance that you will rejoice in His name forever, when you stand in glory and see Him face to face.

For Reflection:
What *does* the name of Jesus mean to you?

---

48 John Newton, "How Sweet the Name of Jesus Sounds" (1779).

How sweet the name of Jesus sounds
In a believer's ear!
It soothes our sorrows, heals our wounds,
And drives away our fear.

It makes the wounded spirit whole
And calms the troubled breast;
'Tis manna to the hungry soul,
And to the weary, rest.

O Jesus, Shepherd, Guardian, Friend,
My Prophet, Priest, and King,
My Lord, my Life, my Way, my End,
Accept the praise I bring.

How weak the effort of my heart,
How cold my warmest thought;
But when I see You as You are,
I'll praise You as I ought.

Till then I would Your love proclaim
With every fleeting breath;
And may the music of Your name
Refresh my soul in death.

"How Sweet the Name of Jesus Sounds"
John Newton

14. A SUPERNATURAL HISTORY

"In those days a decree went out from Caesar Augustus that all the world should be registered. This was the first registration when Quirinius was governor of Syria. And all went to be registered, each to his own town. And Joseph also went up from Galilee, from the town of Nazareth, to Judea, to the city of David, which is called Bethlehem, because he was of the house and lineage of David, to be registered with Mary, his betrothed, who was with child. And while they were there, the time came for her to give birth."

LUKE 2:1-6

In the first chapter of the Gospel of Luke, no sooner has the author introduced himself as a detail-oriented historian than we are immediately ushered into an environment filled with supernatural occurrences. The story of Jesus' birth is filled with angels, predictions, and miracles—and when Luke reports these events, he offers them not as imaginative stories or poetical speculations but as real events: as history.

In our day and age, it is trendy to be seeking truth but taboo to say we have found it. Our culture would have us believe that while it's fine to offer a concept or an idea, we shouldn't say we have certainty. Luke was different. He wasn't satisfied with anything less than knowing with certainty—for himself and for others.

This is why, amid the supernatural occurrences, Luke provides us with political, social, geographical, and historical observations. They may seem quite mundane, but they all matter. We are being shown that all of these events took place in real, historical time. While people back then didn't have Google or social media, they would have known who had served as governor and when. They could have gone to the record of public registration and looked up Joseph's name. The Gospel writer was not providing a philosophy, an idea, or even a religion. Luke, with every word and every detail, made it very clear that Jesus' story doesn't exist in a vacuum.

First- and second-century historians were in no doubt concerning Jesus' reality. Tacitus, a Roman historian who was writing in the early second century, had no interest in supporting the claims of Christ but was absolutely convinced that Jesus was not mythological.[49] Josephus, a Jewish historian writing in AD 93, affirmed the fact that the life, death, and resurrection of Jesus were proclaimed by His followers.[50]

---

49 Tacitus, *Annals*, 15.44.
50 Josephus, *Antiquities of the Jews*, 18.3.3.

The point is this: When we read that Mary laid her firstborn son in a manger, she really did. When we read that the child she gave birth to was conceived through the power of the Holy Spirit, He really was. These supernatural elements are an intrinsic part of the Gospel's account, and Luke's inclusion of historical detail is to underline his claim that his Gospel belongs in the history section, not on the fiction shelf.

Every Christmas season, articles appear in newspapers and magazines that remove the miraculous and promise to reveal the "real" history of the first Christmas. But that cannot be done. Without the supernatural, there is no Christmas, and there is no gospel. The story of the Gospel of Luke is supernatural in its entirety, and not just at its beginning, because it is the story of the Creator of the universe entering into time, revealing Himself as Savior and King. Surely it would be more bizarre if the almighty God did not enter and exit the world in entirely supernatural ways that made mere mortals scratch their heads in amazement! Indeed, in each of the supernatural incidents Luke recorded, we find faithful people who had reflected on the Scriptures and were keenly anticipating that God would break into their environment in a way that had never happened before and would never happen again. When God came, these were the people who were ready for God to come and do what only He could do; these were the people who responded in faith and with awed, joyful amazement.

Christianity is ultimately meaningless apart from the almighty, miraculous intervention of God in time. God has come to meet us, and He did not come to the libraries or lecture halls—to those who work out what is humanly possible or plausible. Nor did He come to the corridors of political power or the palace of the Emperor Augustus. He came to meet us in a cattle shed in Bethlehem. He came to meet us on a Roman cross at Calvary. And, even now, He meets us through His Holy Spirit. He works in ways that we cannot explain and cannot predict. As we considered two days ago, Christmas shows us that God is supernaturally involved in His world. This bears repeating because it cuts against the grain of our culture, which tends to deny the supernatural and decry anyone who is certain about the supernatural. But both the virgin conception and the resurrection from the tomb speak to us of the reality of God's inexplicable activity, and the possibility of certainty about who He is and what He has done. In fact, pride is not found in someone being certain about what they have not seen but which is based on the testimony of God's word; it is found in someone refusing to allow for God breaking into His creation, based on their own mind's incomprehension of how He did it.

The Advent season is a wonderful time to consider the mystery of God's divine work in history. In doing that, our hearts will once again be stirred by the wonder of the supernatural love of the triune God for us, and our eyes will be prepared to see surprising ways in which God is at work in and around us—ways that we cannot explain and have not predicted, but love to enjoy and to praise Him for.

For Reflection:

Are you in any danger of living as though God is not at work supernaturally today?

What difference do you think it would make to your prayers, your decisions, and your perspective on your day to remember that God remains at work in His world?

> *Away in a manger, no crib for a bed,*
> *The little Lord Jesus lay down His sweet head;*
> *The stars in the heavens looked down where*
> *He lay,*
> *The little Lord Jesus asleep on the hay.*
>
> *The cattle are lowing, the Baby awakes,*
> *But little Lord Jesus, no crying He makes.*
> *I love Thee, Lord Jesus, look down from the sky*
> *And stay by my side until morning is nigh.*
>
> *Be near me, Lord Jesus; I ask Thee to stay*
> *Close by me forever, and love me, I pray.*
> *Bless all the dear children in Thy tender care,*
> *And fit us for heaven, to live with Thee there.*
>
> *"Away in a Manger"*
> *Anonymous*

15. SEE AND TELL

"When the angels went away from them into heaven, the shepherds said to one another, 'Let us go over to Bethlehem and see this thing that has happened, which the Lord has made known to us.' And they went with haste and found Mary and Joseph, and the baby lying in a manger. And when they saw it, they made known the saying that had been told them concerning this child."

LUKE 2:15-17

All through his Gospel, Luke makes clear that while people might expect that God would be most interested in those who had status, power, or wealth, the reality is much different. Again and again, God goes for the least, the last, and the left-out. He works in ways and through lives that often take us by surprise.

The shepherds in Luke 2 fit that mold perfectly. We shouldn't glamorize shepherding; it was a difficult, isolating existence. It was not a sought-after vocation. On that first Christmas night, these shepherds were "out in the field, keeping watch over their flock by night."[51] But that didn't last. An angel appeared to them to deliver "good news of great joy" about the birth of the long-expected Messiah, and explained that they would find Him lying in a manger.[52]

The Creator of the universe... in a *manger*?! How could the shepherds believe what they had heard? "Let us go ... and see this thing that has happened, *which the Lord has made known to us*." They realized that they had experienced a divine visitation—a message from the throneroom of heaven—so they proceeded on that basis. And, of course, they found things to be just as the angel had said.

These shepherds went to seek out the one who had come seeking for them. They went to find the dwelling place of the one who had come from heaven to dwell with people such as them:

> *Jesus my Savior to Bethlehem came,*
> *Born in a manger to sorrow and shame;*
> *Oh, it was wonderful—blest be His name!*
> *Seeking for me, for me!*[53]

Only the eye of faith can believe that an angelic announcement was more than a dream, can decide to go look for the Messiah in a manger on that night, or can read this Gospel story and know that it is true. By

---

51 Luke 2:8.
52 Luke 2:9-12.
53 "Seeking for Me" (1878), Anonymous.

nature, our response is to say, *There is no chance that the child who was in that manger is God. There is no chance that the man who was on that middle cross is the Savior of the world.* Only by grace and through faith will the signs that God reveals to us in His word and in His world introduce us to curiosity, and investigation, and then finally, by the power of His Holy Spirit, to true belief and the gift of salvation. So, if you do believe, then get down on your knees before you go to sleep tonight and thank God that He opened your blind eyes, softened your hard heart, and included you in the company of those with whom He is well pleased.

At the first Christmas, God wonderfully took the initiative in grace, and the shepherds responded in faith. They believed the angelic message and eagerly began seeking the manger. Prioritizing their search above their livelihood and all they knew, they immediately sought to see for themselves the Redeemer of the world.

Notice, though, that their faithfulness did not—*could not*—stop when they saw Jesus lying in the manger, just as the angels had promised. "When they saw it, they made known the saying that had been told them concerning this child."[54] In other words, they declared the facts surrounding what God had made known and what they were witnessing.

---

54 Luke 2:17.

We do not know exactly what the shepherds said to others, but it's clear that they couldn't resist sharing what God had revealed; we do not know who they told, but we know that those who heard were left in wonder.[55] What a wonderful illustration of how we are to respond to God's message! True faith doesn't let us keep the enjoyment of God's glory and revelation to ourselves.

The shepherds' declaration fits right in with the message of Luke's entire Gospel: salvation for the whole world is found in Jesus Christ alone. This good news came down in an unlikely fashion to an unlikely group of people in an unlikely setting. And yet, more than 2,000 years later this message is still bringing joy, celebration, and transformation to people all around the world. How like our God!

At the Church of the Nativity in Bethlehem, it's impossible to just stroll in. The door is too low. If you want to enter the place that represents the birth of the Lord Jesus, there is only one way to get in: stoop, bow down, and kneel. This is a beautiful picture of what it looks like to come to Jesus and go and share Jesus. It moves us to ask: *Am I prepared to humble myself before Christ? Am I willing, like those shepherds, to give up my prior assumptions and previous plans to know, follow, and proclaim this Redeemer?*

---

55 Luke 2:18.

After all, what is it that prevents a man or woman from responding to the gospel news like the shepherds did? One word: pride. Pride would have kept the shepherds in the fields, in possession of the angelic announcement but not of a relationship with the Christ. Pride will keep us from coming to Christ on bended knee. Pride will fear mockery or rejection and keep us from sharing Christ with those around us.

Christmas comes alive to the humble. Let's be those who stoop, whose hearts assume a posture of bowing before God's glory and adoring the one who first humbled Himself by coming to us as an infant King. And then let's be those who "go tell it" wherever God has set us and wherever He directs our steps.

For Reflection:

Who are you going to go and tell the gospel to between now and Christmas Day? What issues of pride may prevent you from doing so, and how will you overcome them?

> *Go tell it on the mountain,*
> *Over the hills, and ev'rywhere;*
> *Go, tell it on the mountain*
> *That Jesus Christ is born.*
>
> *While shepherds kept their watching*
> *O'er silent flocks by night,*
> *Behold, throughout the heavens*
> *There shone a holy light.*

The shepherds feared and trembled
When lo, above the earth
Rang out the angel chorus
That hailed our Savior's birth.

Down in a lowly manger
The humble Christ was born,
And God sent us salvation
That blessed Christmas morn.

Go tell it on the mountain,
Over the hills, and ev'rywhere;
Go, tell it on the mountain
That Jesus Christ is born.

"Go, Tell It on the Mountain"
Anonymous

16. WISDOM WORSHIPS

*"After Jesus was born in Bethlehem of Judea in the
days of Herod the king, behold, wise men from the east
came to Jerusalem, saying, 'Where is he who has been
born king of the Jews? For we saw his star when it rose
and have come to worship him.' ... After listening to
the king, they went on their way ... When they saw
the star, they rejoiced exceedingly with great joy. And
going into the house, they saw the child with Mary his
mother, and they fell down and worshiped him."*

MATTHEW 2:1-2, 9-11

We often see this scene depicted on Christmas
cards: a group of wise men coming from the east
in search of the King of the Jews. Yet the appearance
of these men immediately raises several questions. Who
were they? Where did they come from? And why did
they make this journey?

The only description given of these visitors to the
newborn King Jesus is that they were "wise men." They
are called magi in some translations, which indicates
that they studied the movements of the stars. But they
weren't simply astronomers or astrologers. Rather, they

studied the night sky and made theological deductions based on what they found. They were, in a sense, theological scientists. They were serious souls in pursuit of truth, and they desired to see where the evidence they discovered might lead.

And so they arrived in Jerusalem with an inquiry: "Where is he who has been born king of the Jews?" They had come to the conviction that a significant king had been born in Judah, and they traveled a long way to find him. They were deadly serious about uncovering the answer to their question. They would have to be to do as they did! Supposing that they came from Babylon (as is possible, though we cannot know for sure), their journey to Jerusalem would have been approximately 800 miles. It would be one thing to sit around discussing theology at a Babylonian bistro—but what these men did is striking. Confronted by a sign of God's activity in the world, they set out on an arduous journey in search of the truth.

The fact that the wise men had endeavored to discover the truth from their study of the stars is a reminder that an individual's search for God can begin in all kinds of places. The God of the universe, in His grace, uses various means and unusual elements in minds and hearts from all parts of the world in order to lead people to one place: the discovery of the one true God. The three wise men are a standing testimony to the reality of the prophet Jeremiah's announcement: "You will seek me and find me, when you seek me with all your heart."[56]

---

56 Jeremiah 29:13.

How different from these wise men were King Herod and the Jewish religious experts. When Herod heard that they had arrived and were inquiring about the birth of a new King, he assembled the chief priests and scribes, who understood that the Christ was to be born "in Bethlehem of Judea, for so it is written by the prophet."[57] And he was troubled.

This king was the epitome of hostility toward Jesus. He stands for everyone who says to themselves, *I don't mind some religious person sitting quietly in the back seat of my life, but I don't want anybody other than me to be driving the car.* A religious leader who keeps quiet or offers advice is acceptable; one who makes claims on a person's life and who does not agree with what they already think is not. Herod seared his conscience in his attempt to ensure there would be no king to rival him.[58] And, while the outworking is rarely as murderous as his actions were, many do that still today.

The religious specialists, on the other hand, were indifferent to their great knowledge. They were *aware* that Micah had prophesied that the Christ would be born in Bethlehem, but they simply didn't *care.* They worked out for Herod and the wise men where the Scriptures said the long-awaited King of the Jews would be born; but they wouldn't even take the time to make a six-mile journey to meet and worship Him. They were too busy

---

57 Matthew 2:5.
58 Matthew 2:16-18.

with their religion to make time for their rescuing King. These religious experts show that knowing what God's word says is not sufficient. We must allow it to lead us to an encounter with the Lord Jesus.

What moved these wise men, these authorities in their field, to bow down at the cradle of a child? How does that happen? Only by the power of God. And it was they, and not Herod or the priests, who were the ones who "rejoiced exceedingly with great joy."

Having been led by the Scriptures to Jesus, the wise men then made their greatest discovery; and worshiping Christ was the only appropriate response. When they finally encountered Jesus, they fell down, worshiped Him, and offered Him gifts. When our eyes are opened to the majesty of King Jesus, we bow before Him in humility, wonder, and awe.

Presumably Herod, bent on resisting the claims of God on his life, would not have thought these men from the east wise for giving up their time, their energy, and their comforts in order to be in the presence of this newborn King. Likewise the religious experts, bent on their own studies of God's word but refusing to come to the one to whom every part of that word points, would surely have mocked these easterners for giving this child the best gifts they had. You will know plenty of people who likewise consider a life lived wholly and sacrificially for Christ to be a foolish one. But God Himself calls it wise. To worship the one who was born to rule you and save you is to live in line with truth, and to find great joy for this life and for the next. Surely there could be no greater gift.

For Reflection:
How does it comfort you, and how does it challenge you, to consider the truth that God says that the wise life is the one that is lived wholly and sacrificially for Christ?
Do you need to change your priorities or plans in any way?

> *We three kings of Orient are;*
> *Bearing gifts we traverse afar,*
> *Field and fountain, moor and mountain,*
> *Following yonder star.*
>
> *O star of wonder, star of light,*
> *Star with royal beauty bright,*
> *Westward leading, still proceeding,*
> *Guide us to thy perfect Light.*
>
> *Born a King on Bethlehem's plain,*
> *Gold I bring to crown Him again,*
> *King forever, ceasing never,*
> *Over us all to reign.*
>
> *Frankincense to offer have I;*
> *Incense owns a deity nigh;*
> *Prayer and praising, voices raising,*
> *Worshiping God on high.*

Myrrh is mine; its bitter perfume
Breathes a life of gathering gloom;
Sorrowing, sighing, bleeding, dying,
Sealed in the stone-cold tomb.

Glorious now behold Him arise;
King and God and sacrifice:
"Alleluia, alleluia!"
Sounds through the earth and skies.

O star of wonder, star of light,
Star with royal beauty bright,
Westward leading, still proceeding,
Guide us to thy perfect Light.

"We Three Kings of Orient Are"
John H. Hopkins

17. A LIGHT IN
THE DARKNESS

*"The light shines in the darkness, and the darkness
has not overcome it."*

JOHN 1:5

In his 1939 Christmas broadcast to the British nation,
King George VI read from the preamble to a poem by
Minnie Louise Haskins:

> *I said to the man who stood at the gate of the
> year,
> "Give me a light that I may tread safely into the
> unknown."
> And he replied: "Go out into the darkness and
> put your hand into the Hand of God.
> That shall be to you better than light and safer
> than a known way."* [59]

While those words were obviously particularly meaningful to the king and his subjects amid an escalating war

---

59 Minnie Louise Haskins, "God Knows" (1912).

with Germany, they will find an echo in the hearts and minds of men and women today—for we live in a time of great uncertainty and anxiety.

And it is as we consider the darkness of this world that we are all the more ready to celebrate the central message of the Christmas season: the true light has come into the world.[60] And the light is not a philosophy. It's not a political ideology. It's not a sentiment or a concept. The light is a person: Jesus Christ. Jesus came to light our way forward, leading us out of a world of death and into life with Him.

Jesus is the light by which we can see far better than by any would-be light this world might offer. Or, to use Haskins' metaphor, He is the hand of God extended to us. How, then, can we live by His light in a world of darkness?

It's not normal for burglars to call out from the darkness of the yard, "Excuse me, could you turn the spotlights on? I'm trying to steal from your house!" They're burglars! They do their work in the dark. The worst thing that can happen to them is for the lights to come on and reveal them. Similarly, the Bible says that apart from Christ, we are in the dark. We cannot see the truth. We cannot discern what is good. We cannot see sin as sin, or resist doing what is wrong. The fact is that our society is so accustomed to the dark that we often don't even

---

60 John 1:9.

realize the lights are out. As C.S. Lewis wrote, great evil is often "conceived and ordered ... in clean, carpeted, warmed, and well-lighted offices, by quiet men with white collars and cut fingernails and smooth-shaven cheeks who do not need to raise their voice."[61] If we are enabled to see the darkness, we will realize that it is not just present in the obviously bad things happening. It is within our own hearts. It is the natural disposition that says, "I am in charge of me." And it is deeply rooted in everyone—even in the most "upright" people.

At the first Christmas, as the light came and shone in a dark world, it became clear just how dark things were. Herod hated the idea of a king over him because he wanted to be on the throne, and he killed children to resist Jesus. Later in the Gospels, the Pharisees rejected the Messiah because they had their own way of securing salvation, and they killed Jesus Himself. And two thousand years later, still wanting to have the final word over our own lives, still wanting to be the hero of our story, we too, by nature, choose to live in the darkness, despite all the uncertainty and chaos it brings. We spurn the hand that will lead us out of darkness and into light.

But the darkness does not overcome the light.

The work of the Spirit of God is to come into our lives and say, *It's dark in here.* By nature, we don't realize it's dark. By and large, we think it's fine, because it's all

---

61 C.S. Lewis, preface to *The Screwtape Letters* (1961).

we've known. But once we have realized it's dark, we can reach for a light. And light is what Jesus brought and what the Spirit brings.[62]

The Christmas message is fundamentally hopeful. But if it is to be hopeful for us, it must be more than sentimental. Hope turns on the fulcrum of truth. If we would hold on to hope as we look into the coming year, then our own purposes for our lives will do us little good. We can make nothing true by believing it, and we can make nothing right by wanting it. If we would hold on to hope, we need to listen to the voice speaking into our hearts and saying, *It's dark in here,* and pointing us to "the true light," who has come into the world.

So, pause for a moment now. Is the Spirit of God saying of an area of your life, *It's dark here. You need to walk by the light; you need to let Jesus lead you*? Or perhaps you are looking at what next year may hold with anxiety or dread, and the Spirit of God is saying to you, *Put your hand in Jesus' hand, and trust Him to lead you through.* Jesus came into the world to transform us by leading us out of the darkness of self-serving falsehood and into the light of God's true purpose: through many dangers, toils, and snares and out into the glorious light of God's eternal presence. It is as you "put your hand into the Hand of God" that He will prove Himself to be better than the best this world has to offer. Be assured that the light that was born at Christmas still shines in the darkness, and the darkness shall never overcome it.

---

62 2 Corinthians 3:17-18; 4:4.

For Reflection:

As you reflect on the previous paragraph, what might the Spirit of God be saying to you right now?

> *Hark! the herald angels sing,*
> *"Glory to the newborn King:*
> *Peace on earth, and mercy mild,*
> *God and sinners reconciled!"*
> *Joyful, all ye nations, rise,*
> *Join the triumph of the skies;*
> *With th'angelic hosts proclaim,*
> *"Christ is born in Bethlehem!"*
> *Hark! the herald angels sing,*
> *"Glory to the newborn King."*
>
> *Christ, by highest heaven adored,*
> *Christ, the everlasting Lord,*
> *Late in time behold Him come,*
> *Offspring of the Virgin's womb:*
> *Veiled in flesh the Godhead see;*
> *Hail th'incarnate Deity,*
> *Pleased as man with man to dwell,*
> *Jesus, our Immanuel.*
> *Hark! the herald angels sing,*
> *"Glory to the newborn King."*
>
> *Hail the heaven-born Prince of Peace!*
> *Hail the Sun of Righteousness!*
> *Light and life to all He brings,*
> *Risen with healing in His wings.*

Mild He lays His glory by,
Born that man no more may die,
Born to raise the sons of earth,
Born to give us second birth.
Hark! the herald angels sing,
"Glory to the newborn King."

"Hark! The Herald Angels Sing"
Charles Wesley

PART 4

CHRISTMAS
IN THE LETTERS

.

18. I WILL GO THERE

"In these last days [God] has spoken to us by his Son,
whom he appointed the heir of all things, through
whom also he created the world. He is the radiance of
the glory of God and the exact imprint of his nature,
and he upholds the universe by the word of his power.
After making purification for sins, he sat down at the
right hand of the Majesty on high."

HEBREWS 1:2-3

Genesis reminded us that our Creator God is a promise-keeping God. It taught us to expect that He would send someone to restore this fallen world, that this someone is a Deliverer, and that in Him all the nations of the world will be blessed. The Writings and the Prophets provided for us a blurry image full of hope, expectation, and vague details about God's grand plan for redemption. And then the Gospels gave us a crystal-clear lens through which we can see that Jesus is the one in whom all our hopes, all God's promises, all our longings are fulfilled.

Yet still there is far more to consider about Christmas—from the New Testament epistles.

The author of Hebrews, for instance, begins with an introduction that should draw our minds back to the beginning of John's Gospel. God's Son, he reminds his readers, has spoken to His people through His word, is the agent of all creation, inherits everything from the Father, is the perfect expression of God's glory, and upholds the universe by His powerful word. As Prophet, He not only speaks God's words; He *is* God's Word. As Priest, He not only offers a sacrifice for sins, but He himself is the sacrifice. As King, He not only rules His people for a period of time, but He reigns everywhere, forever. And it is He who lay in the manger that first Christmas.

———

As we've noted over our past week of readings, the Gospels of Matthew and Luke introduce us to a whole cast of Christmas characters with whom we've grown quite familiar: Mary, the shepherds, the wise men, and so on. Sometimes we consider those who are less known, such as Zechariah, Elizabeth, Anna, and Simeon. With each passing Christmas season, we have probably been treated to sermons and studies from the perspective of just about every cast member. Yet there is one notable exception: surprisingly few of us have pondered Christmas from Jesus' vantage point. Hebrews offers us a peek at that very perspective. In Hebrews 10:5-6, the author writes:

> *When Christ came into the world, he said,*
> *"Sacrifices and offerings you have not desired,*
> *but a body have you prepared for me; in burnt*

offerings and sin offerings you have taken no pleasure."

Just as Cinderella's glass slipper fit only her foot, these words that Jesus was quoting from Psalm 40 fit nobody but Him.

———

God was preparing for the first Christmas throughout the centuries of the Old Testament, for all the Old Testament sacrifices were mere shadows of the reality to which they pointed. Those sacrifices involved the death of animals that had to be prodded to the altar. They had no choice; they were simply pressed into service. But before He even experienced humanity, Jesus knew His role—His sacrifice—would be different. He willingly consented. In the humblest of forms and in an unexpected setting, God the Son took on a body that was prepared for Him—prepared "as a ransom for many."[63]

The Son looked at this broken world and its sinful people and said to His Father, *Yes, I will go there to be with them. I will become one of them, and I will die for them.* He looked at you and me and said, *Yes, I will make purification for his sins and her sins.* And His Father looked upon Him and said, in a way that no animal being marched to the altar had ever merited, "This is my beloved Son, with whom I am well pleased."[64] The act that most drew

---

63 Matthew 20:28.
64 Matthew 17:5.

forth the love of the Father for the Son was His voluntary offering of Himself as a sacrifice for our sins.[65]

Jesus entered this world not merely so that there could be a virgin birth in Bethlehem but so we might also experience a virgin birth of faith in our own souls. His plan is not merely that Christmas should have happened long ago but that Christmas, in a sense, should happen today. Through His birth, death, resurrection, and ascension, He perfectly accomplished all that is necessary for sinful men and women to experience a miraculous new birth and enter into fellowship with God. And after doing so, "he sat down at the right hand of the Majesty on high."

This is very different from the promise of mere religion, in which rules and effort become futile mechanisms for trying to climb into heaven. In contrast, the manger's message is one of liberating mercy. God has wonderfully taken the initiative and come down to rescue us through Jesus. We don't need to make a long journey to find God, because Christ, the newborn King, knew His role. What is the right response? Simply to bow before Him humbly, praise Him wholeheartedly, and wait for Him expectantly all of our days, being assured of this: because He said, *I will go there to be with them*, you can say, *I will go there to be with Him*.

For Reflection:
How have these truths encouraged your heart today?
What will waiting expectantly for Jesus look like for you?

---

65 John 10:17.

Child in the manger,
Infant of Mary;
Outcast and stranger,
Lord of all;
Child who inherits
All our transgressions,
All our demerits
On Him fall.

Once the most holy
Child of salvation
Gently and lowly
Lived below;
Now as our glorious
Mighty Redeemer,
See Him victorious
O'er each foe.

Prophets foretold Him,
Infant of wonder;
Angels behold Him
On His throne;
Worthy our Savior
Of all our praises;
Happy forever
Are His own.

"Child in the Manger"
Mary MacDougall MacDonald,
trans. by Lachlan Macbean

19. THE GIFT OF ADOPTION

*"When the fullness of time had come, God sent forth
his Son, born of woman, born under the law, to
redeem those who were under the law, so that we
might receive adoption as sons. And because you are
sons, God has sent the Spirit of his Son into our hearts,
crying, 'Abba! Father!' So you are no longer a slave, but
a son, and if a son, then an heir through God."*

GALATIANS 4:4-7

Christmas, is, quite literally, all about family. But not primarily about our human families, wonderful though it is to look back on joyful gatherings around the tree or the table in the past, or to look forward to being in the same room as various family members this year. No—Christmas is about God's family. The whole purpose of God sending forth His Son was "so that we might receive adoption as sons."

As we've seen, Jesus stands out among, and apart from, all other figures of religion, history, and humanity because He alone possesses the qualifications to be the Savior of our world. His coming isn't regarded by the apostle Paul as an accidental intervention; it was a divine appointment. When Paul says that "God sent forth his Son," it's a reminder that Jesus was sent out from a previous state of existence. Jesus' life didn't begin when He was "born of woman" as a child in Bethlehem; He is and was and forever will be. Time cannot bind Him. Without ceasing to be what He was—namely, God—He became what He was not—namely, a man.

He was "born under the law," owing the Father full and perfect obedience—which He, alone in the great mass of humanity through the ages, achieved. And He died in our place, to redeem us. If God would save, then the Savior must be God. If man must bear the punishment because man sinned, then the Savior must be a man. If the man who bears the punishment of sin must himself be sinless, then who other than Jesus Christ meets these qualifications?

> *There was no other good enough*
> *To pay the price of sin;*
> *He only could unlock the gate*
> *Of heav'n and let us in.*[66]

---

66 Cecil Frances Alexander, "There Is a Green Hill Far Away" (1848).

But God did not send His Son simply to save us, glorious though that is. He sent Him to save us so that He could adopt us. This is even more glorious:

> *"Adoption is … the highest privilege that the gospel offers … To be right with God the Judge is a great thing, but to be loved and cared for by God the Father is greater."* [67]

In the Roman world, rich or powerful men would sometimes adopt a boy to be their heir. The adopted son stood to inherit everything from his adoptive parent. Still today, the moment a child is adopted, their whole life changes; they get a new name, a new family, a new home, and often an entirely new way of life.

Yet while such an adoption may be legally official, the legality can exist without the child feeling a true sense of belonging to the family. It often takes time for subjective experience to catch up with objective reality. It's one thing for a child to come and live in a home; it's another, deeper reality to fully experience and express the knitting together of a family—to call one's new parents "Mommy" and "Daddy."

The same is true of our spiritual adoption when we profess faith in Jesus Christ. While our adoption changes our status, it does not immediately and completely change our character. God, however, thankfully isn't satisfied with a simple name change. He wants us to know

---

67 J.I. Packer, *Knowing God* (InterVarsity Press UK, 2023), p 212, 214.

what it means to be His sons and daughters. He longs for us to have the experiential wonder of thinking of Him as our heavenly Father. To do this, He "has sent the Spirit of his Son" to live in our hearts, enabling us to see our relationship to Him as that of child and Father.

The Christian experience isn't simply a legal transaction. Salvation is not just the forgiveness of sins; it is also the welcoming of Spirit-empowered transformation. What Jesus accomplished outwardly on the cross, the Spirit continues inwardly in our hearts. We are rescued, accepted, adopted, and loved. With this change, we can anticipate devotion, passion, tears, enlightenment, involvement, and, ultimately, praise.

All of us are apt to forget our new status as God's children. When we do, the Spirit stands waiting to testify, *No, you truly are His! You've been bought at the greatest price. You are loved and cherished.* When we haven't done as God would have us do—when we're feeling bruised, broken, and discouraged—the Spirit helps us cry, *O Father, Father, could You please help me?* Such pleas should serve as reminders of the wonder of Jesus' finished work. "When the fullness of time had come," He took on flesh so that He could be our redeeming sacrifice and pour out His Spirit to live within our hearts. Without Jesus, our hearts could never cry, "Abba! Father!" Because of Him, our hearts always can.

God seals our adoption as sons and daughters not by some peculiar sign or gift but by the persuasive witness of His Spirit. As we talk to God in prayer, hear from Him through His word, and walk with Him in life, we grow in awareness of His power and His work within us. Because we have been freed from sin's curse and have been given the blessing of adoption, we can cry out to God, adoring Him and worshiping Him in spirit and in truth.

It was for all this that Jesus was born at just the right time: God sent His Son to this world to live, to die, and to rise so that you could become His child, enjoying the intimacy and security of relationship that Jesus has with His Father. Whatever you are doing today, and however you are feeling today, you can know this: if you are Christ's, you are adopted; and if you are adopted, then you are loved with a divine love so deep that eternity is too short for you to plumb it.

For Reflection:
Have you considered before that divine adoption is the greatest wonder of the gospel?
What difference will knowing that you have a divine Father, who loves you and whose world this is, make to the way you look at your day today?

> *See, amid the winter's snow,*
> *Born for us on earth below,*
> *See the tender Lamb appears,*
> *Promised from eternal years.*

Hail, thou ever blessed morn!
Hail, redemption's happy dawn!
Sing through all Jerusalem,
"Christ is born in Bethlehem."

Lo, within a manger lies
He who built the starry skies;
He who, throned in height sublime,
Sits amid the cherubim!

Say, ye holy shepherds, say,
What's your joyful news today?
Wherefore have ye left your sheep
On the lonely mountain steep?

"As we watched at dead of night,
Lo! We saw a wondrous light;
Angels singing, 'Peace on earth'
Told us of the Savior's birth."

Sacred Infant, all divine,
What a tender love was Thine,
Thus to come from highest bliss
Down to such a world as this!

Hail, thou ever blessed morn!
Hail, redemption's happy dawn!
Sing through all Jerusalem,
"Christ is born in Bethlehem."

"See Amid the Winter's Snow"
Edward Caswall

20. HE EMPTIED HIMSELF

"Have this mind among yourselves, which is yours in Christ Jesus, who, though he was in the form of God, did not count equality with God a thing to be grasped, but emptied himself, by taking the form of a servant, being born in the likeness of men."

PHILIPPIANS 2:5-8

Jesus is eternally, truly, and totally God: "the radiance of the glory of God and the exact imprint of his nature"—the complete and perfect "form of God" throughout eternity past.[68]

That reality makes what Paul writes here in Philippians 2 all the more staggering.

Jesus—this divine, preincarnate Son of God—"did not count equality with God a thing to be grasped, but emptied himself..." In other words, instead of holding on to His own uninterrupted glory, He chose to set it aside, and although He was under no obligation to do

---

68 Hebrews 1:3.

so, He came to our fallen, helpless world—and He did so on our behalf. He made Himself nothing, becoming a servant to His own creation. The Christ-child's sign that first Christmas was not a chariot but a manger; it was not a scepter but a stable. He became as much an earthly servant as He had been (and is) a heavenly sovereign. From all appearances, He was nothing more than a mere man.

What does it mean—and what does it not mean—to say that Jesus "emptied himself"? Well, it can't mean that Jesus ceased to be God, or gave up some of His divine attributes, because Matthew tells us in his Gospel that Jesus' birth "took place to fulfill what the Lord had spoken by the prophet: 'Behold, the virgin shall conceive and bear a son, and they shall call his name Immanuel' (which means, God with us)."[69] Although He "emptied himself," Jesus was still 100 percent "God with us"! He was not somebody who *appeared* to be God with us; He *actually was* God with us.

So what *does* Paul mean? "Emptied himself" is not the end of the sentence, and the next two words describe another aspect of the same action: Jesus "emptied himself, by taking..." The "emptying" and the "taking" are linked. Alec Motyer, who was a wonderful scholar and a good friend of mine, once suggested that it is more helpful to ask, "Into what did He empty Himself?" than "What did He empty Himself of?" Asking the question in that first way enables us to see that it was what the

---

69 Matthew 1:22-23.

Lord Jesus *took to* Himself that humbled Him, not what He *laid aside*. It was in taking to Himself *humanity* that He became nothing.

Now, none of us knows the mind of God, and there's no illustration or analogy that can really help us comprehend what He has done, but think about this: if you were God, to come down a natural birth canal, to be born in the way Jesus was born, to live as an outcast, to die as a stranger, to bear the abuse and the ultimate curse of the law… that sounds a lot like becoming "nothing."

Jesus ate, He drank, He worked, He slept, He relaxed—just like everybody else. Yet although He was "in the likeness of men," He was not *merely* what He appeared to be. There was something more about Him. He proved His humanity from His birth until His death. But He also proved His deity throughout those same days. Think about the way He could control the wind and the waves by His word. Think about how He brought the dead back to life.

At the heart of Christmas is the truth that Jesus is both fully God and fully man. And so we must avoid two equal and opposite dangers. Some of us are in danger of so deifying Christ that we don't have a human Christ at all. Others of us are so preoccupied with His humanity that we might lose sight of His divinity. The Scriptures, however, hold both in perfect tension. And it is as we do likewise that we are brought to marvel at this God, who would become "nothing" by becoming a creature—by taking on human flesh.

When the great fifth-century theologian Augustine of Hippo was asked, "What are the central principles of the Christian life?" he replied (and I'm paraphrasing somewhat), "Number one is humility, number two is humility, and number three is humility."[70] At the very heart of Philippians 2 is a call to humility. The apostle Paul points to Christ taking on flesh as the pinnacle of humility, and then he essentially says, *Your attitude should be the Christmas attitude.* Jesus did not approach the incarnation asking, *What's in it for Me?* so much as *What do they need Me to do for them?* He approached the incarnation saying, *Because they matter so much to Me, I will live as if I don't matter. I will lay down My life for them.*

He who was somebody became a nobody so that we who are nobodies might in Christ become somebodies. Jesus must never be less than our Savior, but He is also our example. What the church requires—what this world requires—is not that we would seek to be somebodies but that we would embrace being nobodies who have crucified their egos and found their new identity in Christ alone. Here is our God—the God who became a servant for the sake of others. We are called to marvel at this truth, and then to do likewise.

---

70 Augustine, *Letter 118*, trans. Wilfrid Parsons, FOTC 18 (The Catholic University of America Press, 1953), p 282.

For Reflection:

Do you tend to focus too little on Jesus' deity or His humanity? What difference might a greater focus make to your relationship with Him?

How will today's reading shape the way you view serving others?

> *Once in royal David's city*
> *Stood a lowly cattle shed,*
> *Where a mother laid her baby*
> *In a manger for His bed:*
> *Mary was that mother mild,*
> *Jesus Christ her little Child.*
>
> *He came down to earth from heaven*
> *Who is God and Lord of all,*
> *And His shelter was a stable,*
> *And His cradle was a stall:*
> *With the poor, and meek, and lowly,*
> *Lived on earth our Savior holy.*
>
> *And our eyes at last shall see Him,*
> *Through His own redeeming love;*
> *For that Child so dear and gentle*
> *Is our Lord in heav'n above,*
> *And He leads His children on*
> *To the place where He is gone.*

Not in that poor lowly stable,
With the oxen standing by,
We shall see Him, but in heaven,
Set at God's right hand on high;
When like stars His children crowned
All in white shall wait around.

"Once in Royal David's City"
Cecil Frances Alexander

21. CHRISTMAS IN ELEVEN WORDS

"The grace of God has appeared,
bringing salvation for all people."
TITUS 2:11

The story of Christmas—the story of Jesus—is the most beautiful story that the world has ever been privileged to hear. It is surely partly on account of its wonder and beauty that about a third of the world's population will at least pay lip service to it over the next few days. Nevertheless, many around the globe have not heard the name of Jesus and the message of the gospel; many don't believe that the Jesus of the Christmas narrative is truly the Jesus of history; and many think either that Jesus is just one path among many to follow or that there is a better path.

If we are going to be well equipped to tell others about Jesus, we need to know what the Christmas story is really all about. Sometimes we have ten minutes to explain the gospel to a neighbor or family member over the Christmas period. Other times, though, we have no more than ten seconds. And Paul helpfully summarizes the glory of the Christmas story in eleven words in his letter to Titus: "The grace of God has appeared, bringing salvation for all people." The Greek word for "appeared" is *epephánē*, which gives us our English word "epiphany." *There has been an epiphany,* says Paul, *and it's God Himself who has graciously appeared to bring salvation.*

God's grace—His undeserved kindness—appeared when Jesus was born as a Savior because this is a world in need of salvation. He appeared not because of our great performance but because of our great need. Even there on that first evening, as baby Jesus was asleep in that manger, the shadow of the cross was already cast over the cradle.

Jesus was a man with a mission. He was the bridge over the troubled waters of our alienation, emptiness, rebellion, and indifference. The Christmas story is a great story because it is the gospel story—the good news of what God, in His overwhelming and undeserved kindness, has done to save His people. It is a beautiful story. It is a compelling story. And it is a life-changing story. So why doesn't everyone believe it?

In my experience, four common sentiments prevent men and women from embracing the grace of God that has appeared in the coming of the Son of God.

First, we are not honest with ourselves or with others. We are prone to run from questions or concerns that are deeper than surface level. We can get fixated on our self-worth—we want to be boosted, not humbled—and challenging that worth has become one of the great social heresies of our age. So the idea that an individual is, as the Bible says, a rebel against God's rule, guilty in His sight and facing condemnation does not go down well. Salvation only makes sense if it is for people who need a rescue, but this does not fit with our modern sense of ourselves as basically good and fundamentally able to solve our problems.

Second, our understanding of tolerance has become unmoored from how the Bible sees it. It is important to practice tolerance, patience, and love so that we can live peaceably with those who oppose our thinking. We never know when God might use our kindness to woo someone to Himself. But it is a quantum leap from that type of tolerance to the contemporary wisdom which suggests that all views are equally valid and that no one can speak with certainty concerning truth or moral absolutes.

Third, many of us buy into the lie that we can work it out. We think we can work with God as though He's a business partner—any success is down to both of us. Or we think we will earn His favor through our good works—any achievement is down to us. "The grace of God has appeared" will not have the slightest semblance of meaning to those who are relying on their own efforts rather than His kindness.

Fourth, we mistakenly think that God will forgive us because it's His job. Fueled at Christmas time by sentimentalism and the fact that Santa always does come with presents, however naughty a child has been, we take the view (perhaps unconsciously) that God is obliged to love us and accept us. Forgiveness is what He does. But while forgiveness is freely offered, it must be received. God demands nothing but that we accept who He is and who we are and who is therefore to be calling the shots in our lives—that we repent. We cannot receive forgiveness into our hands if we keep our rightful Ruler at arm's length.

This, then, is why the Christmas gospel is so wonderful yet so rejected. For all four of these groups, however, there is hope. We have the joy and privilege of being able to tell those around us:

> *There is one who died for you, in part to show you just how much you are worth to Him—a sense of worth that you will never muster up from yourself, but one that lies in being humble.*

> *There is one who has said and proven that He is "the way, and the truth, and the life," bringing clarity to the biggest questions of our lives and, therefore, peace as we make our biggest decisions.*[71]

> *There is one who has said, "It is finished" as He completed the work only He could do, so that you*

---

71 John 14:6.

> *do not need to wonder if you have done enough
> for God, and veer between pride and anxiety.*[72]
>
> *There is one who has offered a forgiveness to
> all—if we will confess with our mouths and
> believe in our hearts that He is the risen Lord of
> all, including of our lives.*[73]

No one will understand the joy of Christmas until they understand the necessity of Christmas. The grace of God has appeared, bringing salvation to all people. Perhaps there will be someone today, or over the coming week, whose eternity could be changed by the ten seconds it will take you to share that Christmas truth with them.

For Reflection:
Who will you pray for, that you have an opportunity to share this eleven-word summary of the gospel with them this week? Which of the four reasons for rejecting the gospel do you think that person is most likely to struggle with, and how might you help them think that through?

> *O holy night! The stars are brightly shining;
> It is the night of the dear Savior's birth.
> Long lay the world in sin and error pining,
> Till He appeared and the soul felt its worth.
> A thrill of hope—the weary world rejoices,
> For yonder breaks a new and glorious morn!*

---

72 John 19:30.
73 Romans 10:9.

Fall on your knees! O hear the angel voices!
O night divine, O night when Christ was
born!
O night divine! O night, O night divine!

Led by the light of faith serenely beaming,
With glowing hearts by His cradle we stand.
So led by light of a star sweetly gleaming,
Here came the wise men from Orient land.
The King of kings lay thus in lowly manger,
In all our trials born to be our Friend.
He knows our need—to our weakness is no
stranger.
Behold your King, before Him lowly bend!
Behold your King, before Him lowly bend!

Truly he taught us to love one another;
His law is love, and His gospel is peace.
Chains shall He break, for the slave is our
brother,
And in His name all oppression shall cease.
Sweet hymns of joy in grateful chorus raise
we;
Let all within us praise His holy name.
Christ is the Lord! O praise His name
forever!
His pow'r and glory evermore proclaim!
His pow'r and glory evermore proclaim!

"O Holy Night"
Placide Cappeau, trans. by John S. Dwight

22. THE CRADLE AND THE CROSS

"In this is love, not that we have loved God
but that he loved us and sent his Son to be the
propitiation for our sins."

1 JOHN 4:10

Why do so many of us anticipate Christmas each year with such delight? For the believer, the answer ought surely to lie, above all, in the awareness that Jesus Christ came to take away our sins. If we say that God has shown His love for us in the incarnation, that is accurate—but insufficient. John did not write "In this is love, not that we have loved God but that he loved us and sent his Son," only to bring his sentence to a full stop; he continued it, reminding us that God "sent his Son *to be the propitiation for our sins.*" Jesus was sent into this world to die, not only to live—to go to the cross, not only to lie in the manger. Leaning on the old hymn "O Love That Wilt Not Let Me Go" as our guide, let's consider three takeaways from this short but theologically weighty Bible verse.[74]

The love of God for us is, first, an initiative-taking love that will not let you go. It is something that is graciously revealed to us and is discovered by us. It's a bit of a mystery, really. It is not something that we can conjure up by ourselves. It is not that we have been sent out into the world to try and engage with divinity; no, rather something far more wonderful has happened. *This is love,* John says, *that God has taken the initiative in Christ.* And God then invites us to accept His free gift of salvation.

In the book of Jude, there's an amazing juxtaposition between an exhortation to "keep yourselves in the love of God," and a wonderful reminder that God will "keep you from stumbling and … present you blameless before the presence of his glory with great joy."[75] It's a reminder that a loving relationship takes two. If God is your friend and has embraced you, then He will not let you go. But even the most loving embrace is uncomfortable if one party is fighting it, constantly trying to turn away.

Jesus, on one occasion, said of His followers, "I give them eternal life, and they will never perish, and no one will snatch them out of my hand."[76] And we might add that we are not strong enough to jump out of His hand

74 George Matheson, "O Love That Wilt Not Let Me Go" (1882).
75 Jude 21, 24.
76 John 10:28.

when He has determined to keep us to the very end. His love is a love that will not let us go; it's a love that led the old Scottish farmer to pray on a daily basis, "Dear Lord, keep me kept."

⸺

Second, God shines a "light that follows all my way." So much throughout Scripture has to do with light and darkness. The apostle Paul clearly and pointedly describes Christians using the imagery of light and dark: "At one time you were darkness, but now you are light in the Lord."[77] He doesn't say, "At one time you *lived in* darkness" but "At one time you *were* darkness." That's quite a judgment. By nature, we are darkness, and we need God to shine into our darkness, to show us the extent of our depravity, and to flood us with His life-giving light. And when that floodlight does shine forth, we become living testimonies of Isaiah's prophecy that we studied a couple of weeks ago: "The people walking in darkness have seen a great light; those who dwelt in a land of deep darkness, on them has light shone."[78] And, as we considered on December 7th, Jesus Himself is "the light of men" and the one who "shines in the darkness," so that "whoever follows [him] will not walk in darkness, but will have the light of life."[79]

⸺

77 Ephesians 5:8.
78 Isaiah 9:2.
79 John 1:4-5; 8:12.

Third and finally, God alone grants lasting joy that can "seekest me through pain." One of the real challenges of Christmas's commercialization is that there are so many temptations and inducements to try to hide any sense of pain, disappointment, regret, or sorrow. We think we can push it all down for now and just have a little more eggnog, play some festive music, eat some more treats, or dance to a favorite carol. We are told that this is a season of joy, without being reminded where that joy is to be found. The trouble with that is that there is no form of easy escapism that can deal with the pain all of us face at some point in life. There's a reason why Jesus was "a man of sorrows and acquainted with grief"—because that is the way of this fallen world.[80] Yet that was not the only reason—for it was also so that He might bear *our* sorrows and griefs, by bearing *our* sin, so that you and I may be acquainted with eternal joy.

All this is why, again and again, we have noted that Christmas and Easter—the cradle and the cross—cannot be rightly understood apart from each other. God demonstrated His love for us not simply by sending Jesus as a baby in Bethlehem so that He could grow up and show us how to live a good life; rather, "God shows his love for us in that while we were still sinners, Christ *died* for us."[81]

---

80 Isaiah 53:3.
81 Romans 5:8.

The pressures and busyness of the Christmas season often bring out the worst in us. Rare is the man or woman who would say that he or she has not struggled with envy or deceit or anger and has not spoken bitter or impatient or impure words through December! But the word of God comes to us and reminds us that this is the very reason for Christmas—that Jesus was born so that He might die. Here is the good news: in this is love, that Christ appeared in this world to take away every last one of your sins. So today, lay hold of this message of love, light, and joy with renewed gratitude. And let these words be the highlight of your Christmas season: "He loved us and sent his Son to be the propitiation for our sins."

For Reflection:
How might you make sure that you call this verse to mind each day for the rest of December?

> *O Love that wilt not let me go,*
> *I rest my weary soul in thee.*
> *I give thee back the life I owe,*
> *That in thine ocean depths its flow*
> *May richer, fuller be.*
>
> *O Light that follows all my way,*
> *I yield my flick'ring torch to thee.*
> *My heart restores its borrowed ray,*
> *That in thy sunshine's blaze its day*
> *May brighter, fairer be.*

O Joy that seekest me through pain,
I cannot close my heart to thee.
I trace the rainbow through the rain,
And feel the promise is not vain,
That morn shall tearless be.

O Cross that liftest up my head,
I dare not ask to fly from thee.
I lay in dust, life's glory dead,
And from the ground there blossoms red,
Life that shall endless be.

"O Love That Wilt Not Let Me Go"
George Matheson

PART 5

AWAITING A
NEW ADVENT

.

23. YOUR KINGDOM COME

*"Then the seventh angel blew his trumpet, and there
were loud voices in heaven, saying, 'The kingdom of
the world has become the kingdom of our Lord and of
his Christ, and he shall reign forever and ever.'"*

REVELATION 11:15

In one sense, the whole of Scripture is both a lesson in
history and a promise for the future, in order that we
may become like Jesus and glorify Him in the present.
It's often been said that in the Old Testament Jesus is
predicted, in the Gospels He is revealed, in Acts He is
preached, in the Epistles He is explained, and in the
book of Revelation He is expected. It is to that book of
great expectation that we'll turn today and tomorrow.

When we dipped our toes into Abraham's story in
Genesis, Solomon's dedication of the temple in 2 Chronicles, and the prophecies from Isaiah and Micah, we saw
how each pointed forward to Jesus. We look back to stories and prophecies such as those and realize that Christ
is not merely another priest for His people but is the
Great High Priest and sacrificial Lamb of God; He is
not merely another prophet but the very Word of God;

and He is not merely another earthly ruler but the eternal King of kings and Lord of lords.

But between the prophecies and their fulfillment, God's people had to wait.

⁓

Because we have the benefit of seeing how Jesus was the "yes" to all the promises and shadows of the Old Testament, it is easy to forget that many generations came and went during the intertestamental period's four centuries of divine "silence." After the prophetic ministry of Malachi, God's people heard nothing new from Him and were subject to a variety of foreign rulers. The kingdom of Israel was a faint memory and a future promise. There was a remnant of faithful believers that would have raised their families in the ways of the Lord, but their children and grandchildren surely heard the stories and prophecies and asked questions like *Dad, when is the Messiah coming?* or *Grandma, do you really think the Lord will send our people a great King?* or *Uncle, how will the kingdom ever really be restored?*

So when we get into the New Testament—when John the Baptist arrives ahead of Jesus to announce that "the kingdom of heaven is at hand"[82]—the beneficiaries of the predicted and prophesied material had to try to make sense of what it would mean for God to establish a kingdom for His people, and what the King of that kingdom would do and be like. Almost without

---

82 Matthew 3:2.

exception, when Jesus began to speak about the kingdom, people thought of it in terms of political revolution and national restoration for Israel. They thought of it in geographical and political terms. They failed to understand that, ultimately, what Jesus was speaking about was a kingdom that was not "of this world" or "from the world," but a kingdom that is first and foremost spiritual and eternal rather than national and territorial.[83] What was God's Son doing when He entered this world as a newborn King? He was beginning to show the world how He would put together a kingdom of people from every tribe, nation, and language.[84]

This establishment of Jesus' kingdom takes place in three ways: the kingdom has come, is coming, and will come.

The kingdom *has come already* in the person and works of Jesus, who announced, "The time is fulfilled, and the kingdom of God is at hand."[85] What are the miracles of Jesus except the emblems of the King's activity in and through His creation? He who created the DNA of every individual has no difficulty in giving sight to the blind, making the lame walk, or raising the dead to life.

The kingdom *is coming* as the Holy Spirit awakens the souls of men and women, transferring them from the kingdom of darkness into the kingdom of light. How does that take place? By gospel proclamation that makes

---

83 John 18:36.
84 Revelation 7:9.
85 Mark 1:15.

disciples, just as Jesus commanded His earliest followers before He ascended into heaven.[86]

Finally, the kingdom *will come* at some God-ordained, undisclosed time, when He will make all things new. The first advent of Jesus saw the coming of the King to display the kingdom and open the kingdom; the second advent of Jesus will see the final arrival of His kingdom in all its fullness of glory. It is to that advent that the book of Revelation looks.

As we read in Revelation 11 about the final of seven trumpet calls, it is as if God is speaking to us from a future day to remind us of our hope in this life and for this world: "The kingdom of the world has become the kingdom of our Lord and of his Christ, and he shall reign forever and ever." When we look around, turn on the news, or scroll through social media, we can remember that things won't always be this way. All that is wrong will be made right; and even the best of this life will be made better! Remembering that the kingdom is yet to come means we do not settle for the best of what this world has to offer, nor do we despair over the worst that this world throws at us. One day, all this will be swallowed up by the glorious reign of the Lord Jesus. That is our true home, and that will be the moment of our greatest celebration.

When we think about Jesus Christ's advent, we do our hearts and minds a disservice if we think only of the first

---

86 Matthew 28:18-20.

and not the second. Christmas isn't only a celebration of what our newborn King came down to earth to save us *from*; it's a celebration of what He came to save us *for*— eternal life with Him in His perfected kingdom. Christ's kingship matters. It mattered in the manger. It matters today. And it will matter forever.

For Reflection:

What difference does it make to our successes and failures, and to our response to the joys and sorrows this world brings, to know…

• the kingdom has come, in the past?
• the kingdom is coming, in the present?
• the kingdom will come, in the future?

Which aspect of the kingdom do you want to particularly meditate on and enjoy today?

> *Good Christian men, rejoice*
> *With heart and soul and voice;*
> *Give ye heed to what we say:*
> *Jesus Christ was born today.*
> *Ox and ass before Him bow,*
> *And He is in the manger now.*
> *Christ is born today!*
> *Christ is born today!*
>
> *Good Christian men, rejoice*
> *With heart and soul and voice;*
> *Now ye hear of endless bliss:*
> *Jesus Christ was born for this!*

He has opened heaven's door,
And man is blest forevermore.
Christ was born for this!
Christ was born for this!

Good Christian men, rejoice
With heart and soul and voice;
Now ye need not fear the grave:
Jesus Christ was born to save!
Calls you one and calls you all
To gain His everlasting hall.
Christ was born to save!
Christ was born to save!

"Good Christian Men, Rejoice"
Trans. by John M. Neale

24. LOOKING FORWARD

*"Then I saw a new heaven and a new earth, for
the first heaven and the first earth had passed
away, and the sea was no more. And I saw the holy
city, new Jerusalem, coming down out of heaven
from God, prepared as a bride adorned for her
husband. And I heard a loud voice from the throne
saying, 'Behold, the dwelling place of God is with
man ... He will wipe away every tear from their
eyes, and death shall be no more, neither shall
there be mourning, nor crying, nor pain anymore,
for the former things have passed away.'"*

REVELATION 21:1-4

"Will God indeed dwell with man on the earth?"
That was the question that Solomon asked in
2 Chronicles 6, way back (as it were) on December 6th.
And from our 21st-century vantage point, we can see
how God has dwelt with man on the earth—in the gar-
den, in the tabernacle, in the temple, in the person of
Jesus, and through His Spirit. He truly is Immanuel—
God with us.

Throughout this Advent season, we have been trying to get the big picture of how the Bible fits together as it relates to Christmas. And our focus today, as yesterday, is to ask, *How does this story end? What will it look like for God finally and fully to dwell with His people?*

In the early fifth century, Augustine provided for the church what was essentially the first philosophy of history from a Christian perspective. It took him 13 years to write it, and it remains a classic, even more than 1,500 years later. In this book, *The City of God*, he explains history in terms of one overarching principle: from the fall of humanity to the end of time, there have existed (and will exist) two rival cities, two rival societies, two rival loves. By our nature, we are involved in the city of man, and only by God's grace will we ever forsake that and instead be devoted to the city of God. To quote Augustine, "Two cities have been formed by two loves: the earthly by love of self, even to the contempt of God; the heavenly by the love of God, even to the contempt of self."[87]

This is a stark way to view the world. But when you search the Scriptures and observe the world, it makes sense. In the city of God are the people of God. It is God's place, and it is under God's rule and blessing. The city of man comprises earthly society, established in stubborn independence from God. The former is

---

87 Augustine, *The City of God*, trans. by Marcus Dods, Cambridge Texts in the History of Political Thought (Cambridge UP, 1998), 14.28.

destined to rule the world. The latter is destined to pass away.

God is going to make this world brand-new. He has been preparing it from all of eternity—and when He finally brings it to fruition, no one and nothing will be allowed to spoil it. That is why sin must be punished, justice must be done, and evil must be destroyed. It is a world "in which righteousness dwells" and from which unrighteousness has been cast away forever.[88]

What we read about in Revelation 21:1-4 is a place that is easy to wish for but hard to understand. It is a place where there will be no more crying, no more pain, no more death—even the mere prospect of hurt and loss will be gone. It will be paradise restored. It will be a new garden with a tree of life, but the tree of the knowledge of good and evil will be no more.[89]

When Peter writes concerning Jesus' second advent in 2 Peter 3, he assures his readers that all that was ruined in the old will be repaired and beautified in the new. The word "new" in verse 13 refers not to time and origin but to quality. The fire he speaks of can be seen as a refining fire, that melts the original object so that impurities can be removed and what exists can be made new. In other words, Satan is not going to get the satisfaction of God destroying His creation. Rather, God is going to purify it. He's going to transform it so that it reflects all the glory and magnificence that He intended for it all along.

---

88 2 Peter 3:13.
89 Revelation 2:7; 22:2, 14, 19.

Such a notion preserves the idea of the "earthiness" of the earth. There is a sense in which we need to ground these truths in the fact that not only will there be a new heaven, but there will be a new earth. Our future as God's people is here—but a perfect here. As Isaiah says of God's redeemed people, "They shall not hurt or destroy in all my holy mountain [that is, the New Jerusalem] for the earth shall be full of the knowledge of the LORD as the waters cover the sea."[90]

A new creation will come. That much is plain. A new Jerusalem, "the holy city," will house those whom God redeems. And we will be able to behold a world in which "the dwelling place of God is with man." As believers, we understand that God walked this earth 2,000 years ago. We know God's presence today thanks to His indwelling Holy Spirit, for the church (the people, not the buildings) is God's temple on the earth for now. But our knowledge and experience of Him right now is so limited. When He ushers in the new heavens and the new earth, however, there will be no special place in the new creation where God's presence will be concentrated. There will be no special building we must visit if we want to meet God. There will be no distance between God and us. There will be no temple because *everything* will be temple.[91]

---

90 Isaiah 11:9.
91 Revelation 21:22.

The New Testament ends in the way the Old Testament ends: looking forward with anticipation and confident expectation. That is one of the marks of Christian reality. It is one of the tests of the vibrancy of our faith and the spiritual vitality of our churches. We are a waiting people: waiting not for Christmas but for Christ.

So as another Advent season draws to a close, look forward so that you will continue to be drawn to what lies ahead. Take seriously the challenge of living a life that is pure before God's gaze—that is ready for His return. And foster a passionate concern to see others come to know and love our God, who came down at the first Christmas and is surely, gloriously coming back again.

For Reflection:

What aspect of the new creation are you particularly looking forward to? How does that move you to praise Jesus now and live for Him today?

What tends to stop you from living as though Jesus will return? What could you do in the new year to make sure your eyes look forward more than they look down?

> *Love divine, all loves excelling,*
> *Joy of heav'n to earth come down,*
> *Fix in us Thy humble dwelling;*
> *All Thy faithful mercies crown!*
> *Jesus, Thou art all compassion,*
> *Pure, unbounded love Thou art;*
> *Visit us with Thy salvation;*
> *Enter every trembling heart.*

Breathe, O breathe Thy loving Spirit
Into every troubled breast!
Let us all in Thee inherit,
Let us find the promised rest.
Take away our love of sinning;
Alpha and Omega be;
End of faith, as its beginning,
Set our hearts at liberty.

Come, Almighty to deliver;
Let us all Thy life receive;
Suddenly return and never,
Nevermore Thy temples leave.
Thee we would be always blessing,
Serve Thee as Thy hosts above;
Pray, and praise Thee without ceasing,
Glory in Thy perfect love.

Finish then, Thy new creation;
Pure and spotless let us be;
Let us see Thy great salvation
Perfectly restored in Thee.
Changed from glory into glory,
Till in heav'n we take our place,
Till we cast our crowns before Thee,
Lost in wonder, love, and praise.

"Love Divine, All Loves Excelling"
Charles Wesley

AFTER CHRISTMAS

(A CURE FOR THE
POST-CHRISTMAS BLUES)

*"My soul magnifies the Lord,
and my spirit rejoices in God my Savior …
he has filled the hungry with good things,
and the rich he has sent away empty."*

LUKE 1:46-47, 53

The few days between Christmas and the New Year teach us something profound about our souls' longings. More often than not, Christmas Day's jubilation and gladness seem to come and go in a flash. After so much anticipation, we can feel as if we are left with little more than ribbons and wrapping, clean-up and returns. Why must Christmas come and go so quickly?!

Pastor and theologian Sinclair Ferguson looks back to his younger self and remembers how…

*"when I was a child, Christmas seemed to die
every year by bedtime on December 25th.*

> *The anticipation seemed long; the realization all too brief. I even tried wrapping up my presents again and opening them the following morning.*"[92]

For children and for adults, the magic of this season of celebration and commotion never lasts, because the day itself only points us toward what C.S. Lewis described as the "deeper magic from before the dawn of time."[93]

⌒————⌒

When Jesus' own mother sang praise to God as she anticipated Christ's birth, she proclaimed, "He has filled the hungry with good things." This has always been the experience of God's people: the psalmist sang of how the Lord "satisfies the longing soul, and the hungry soul he fills with good things."[94] Yet it is not the experience of all people: there have always been those who "wandered in desert wastes" so that "hungry and thirsty, their soul fainted with them."[95] This is our condition apart from Christ: wandering aimlessly "as in a dry and weary land where there is no water."[96] Without Him, relief is beyond reach, and solace and comfort are nothing more than a distant dream.

---

92 Sinclair B. Ferguson, *Child in the Manger: The True Meaning of Christmas* (Banner of Truth, 2015), p 41.
93 C.S. Lewis, *The Lion, the Witch and the Wardrobe* (1950), ch. 15.
94 Psalm 107:9.
95 Psalm 107:4-5.
96 Psalm 63:1.

There isn't a person alive who hasn't felt the pang of unmet expectation and longing. This is simply how God designed us: to yearn and pine for something greater than ourselves. The problem, of course, is that we attempt to meet those longings with something right in front of us. Some of us count on Christmas to fulfill those desires every time the calendar flips from November to December. But Christmas won't cut it. Our longings run deeper than a single merry day or the weeks that accompany it.

The reason that not even the joy of the Christmas season can satisfy us is that our very selves are made for the God who makes Christmas meaningful. If we attempt to live and celebrate apart from Him—and all of us will know the temptation to get caught up in the consumerism of the season!—no amount of holiday cheer can fill the void that's left. As Augustine reminded us, God has made us for Himself, and our hearts are restless until they find their rest in Him.[97]

The good news is that God is in the business of heart transplants, offering new life to His people. He illumines our minds by the truth of the gospel.[98] We no longer need to try and work our way up to some acceptance with God because there is in Christ a righteousness that is credited to us through faith in Him.[99] He sets our hearts free from bondage to sin. He washes clean our inordinate affections, and then He motivates

---

97 Augustine, *Confessions*, 1.1.1.
98 2 Corinthians 4:4-6.
99 Romans 3:22.

and enables us to live in the light of the truth of His word, to discover that His law is, in Christ, a pathway to freedom and joy rather than a restriction.

In other words, God works in such a way that we begin to love what He loves. All this comes from divine heart surgery, when the Almighty fulfills His promise to "remove the heart of stone from your flesh and give you a heart of flesh."[100]

———

According to Mary's song, in an act of divine irony, while God has "filled the hungry with good things … the rich he has sent away empty." Those who have no consciousness of need, who are complacent and insist, "I'm just not hungry," God sends away. But to all who admit their need, who feel their hunger, Jesus declares, "I am the bread of life; whoever comes to me shall not hunger, and whoever believes in me shall never thirst."[101]

The big day is in the past now. All that work of preparation through December (or, perhaps, since September!) has had its culmination. Soon enough, the lights on the houses will come down, the tree will be packed away, and January will be here. And all of that is okay, for we do not live for Christmas but for the one who was born at Christmas. The wonderful thing about being His follower is that what is most wonderful about Christmas Day remains true every day. Jesus is your

---

100 Ezekiel 36:26.
101 John 6:35.

Immanuel. Jesus is the one who gives you all you need—the one who fulfilled every promise of God and fills full every one of His followers. So, with Christmas Day in the rearview mirror and a new year about to dawn, perhaps today is a perfect day to say to your Immanuel, "Jesus, You're the only one who can fill my heart. Above all else—more than the gifts and the food of this season, more than the things I aim to do and be in the year to come—I want Your joy to fill me and strengthen me." Ask Him in faith, and He will surely do it.

the good book
COMPANY

BIBLICAL | RELEVANT | ACCESSIBLE

At The Good Book Company, we are dedicated to helping Christians and local churches grow. We believe that God's growth process always starts with hearing clearly what he has said to us through his timeless word—the Bible.

Ever since we opened our doors in 1991, we have been striving to produce Bible-based resources that bring glory to God. We have grown to become an international provider of user-friendly resources to the Christian community, with believers of all backgrounds and denominations using our books, Bible studies, devotionals, evangelistic resources, and DVD-based courses.

We want to equip ordinary Christians to live for Christ day by day, and churches to grow in their knowledge of God, their love for one another, and the effectiveness of their outreach.

Call us for a discussion of your needs or visit one of our local websites for more information on the resources and services we provide.

Your friends at The Good Book Company

thegoodbook.com | thegoodbook.co.uk
thegoodbook.com.au | thegoodbook.co.nz
thegoodbook.co.in